Anti-Inflammatory Cookbook for Beginners 2023

2000 Days of Quick, Easy and Delicious Recipes to Reduce Inflammation, Balance Hormones and Live healthily | Includes a 40-day Weight-Loss Meal Plan

Rosalinda Sherman

© Copyright 2022 All rights reserved.

The content contained within this book may not be reproduced, duplicated or transmitted without direct written permission from the author or the publisher.

Under no circumstances will any blame or legal responsibility be held against the publisher, or author, for any damages, reparation, or monetary loss due to the information contained within this book. Either directly or indirectly.

Legal Notice:

This book is copyright protected. This book is only for personal use. You cannot amend, distribute, sell, use, quote or paraphrase any part, or the content within this book, without the consent of the author or publisher.

Disclaimer Notice:

Please note the information contained within this document is for educational and entertainment purposes only. All effort has been executed to present accurate, up to date, and reliable, complete information. No warranties of any kind are declared or implied. Readers acknowledge that the author is not engaging in the rendering of legal, financial, medical or professional advice. The content within this book has been derived from various sources. Please consult a licensed professional before attempting any techniques outlined in this book.

By reading this document, the reader agrees that under no circumstances is the author responsible for any losses, direct or indirect, which are incurred as a result of the use of information contained within this document, including, but not limited to, — errors, omissions, or inaccuracies.

Table of Contents

INTRODUCTION: WHAT IS THE DEFINITION OF INFLAMMATION? 8
WHAT ARE THE CONSEQUENCES OF CHRONIC INFLAMMATION? 9
WHAT EXACTLY IS AN ANTI-INFLAMMATORY DIET? 11
BREAKFASTS 12

- Walnut and Banana Bowl 12
- Sweet Potato Oat Bars 12
- Baked Eggs with Portobello Mushrooms 13
- Milk and Creamy Yogurt Bowl 14
- A Quick antipasto pasta 14
- Orange Oatmeal Muffins 15
- Coconut Rice with Berries 15
- Blueberry Breakfast Blend 16
- Golden Milk 16
- Spiced Morning Chia Pudding 16
- Beet and Cherry Smoothie 17
- Breakfast and Brunch Mushroom Crepes 17
- Fruit and Millet Breakfast 18
- Healthy Chia Pudding 18
- Breakfast Porridge 19

Lunch 19

- Lemongrass and Ginger Mackerel 19
- Brown Rice and Shitake Miso Soup with Scallions 20
- Capellini Soup with Tofu And Shrimp 20
- Chicken and Brussels sprouts 21
- Bean Shawarma Salad 21
- Cod and Quinoa Mix 22
- Jicama Black Bean Salad 22
- Cherry-balsamic Chicken Breasts 23
- Creamy Turkey with Mushrooms 23
- Shirataki Pasta with Avocado and Cream 24
- Energy Bites 24
- Banana Pops 25
- Almond-Orange Torte 25
- Raspberry and Chard Smoothie 26

Apple, Berries, and Kale Smoothie 26
Orange Banana Alkaline Smoothie 27
Balsamic Scallops 27
Vegan "Frittata" 27
Beets Gazpacho 28
Baked Butternut Squash Rigatoni 28
Anti-inflammatory Chicken Porridge 29

Dinner 30
Beef, Pork, and Lamb Thai Beef with Coconut Milk 30
Berry Bliss Slow Cooker Pork 30
Fake Mushroom Risotto 31
Chicken with Fennel and Zucchini 31
Rosemary Pork Chops 32
Mushroom Risotto 32
Slow Cooker Shawarma 33
Garlicky Lamb Stew 33
Pork Sausage 34
Yogurt with Dates 34
Chai Pudding 35
Lemon and Mint Breezy Blueberry 35
Spinach Soup with Gnocchi 35
Meatballs 36
Ginger Honey Pork Chops 36
Quick & Juicy Lamb Chops 37
Salmon and Feta Cheese and Papillote 37

Salad 38
Chopped Thai Salad 38
Healthy Tuna Salad 39
Massaged Swiss Chard Salad with Chopped Egg 39
Veggie Salad 40
Grilled Eggplant Salad 40
Blackberry Salad 41
Zucchini Salad 41
Nutritious Salad with Lentil And Beets 41
Carrot and Raisin Salad 42
Pineapple Apple Salad 42

Perfect Chicken Salad 42

Fish and Seafood 43

Tuna and Kale 43

Veggie, Salmon & Quinoa Bowl 43

Baked Cod Fillets with Mushroom 44

Broiled Sea Bass 44

Greek Baked Cod 45

Mussels and Clams in White Wine 46

Spicy Cod 46

Creamy Turmeric Shrimp 47

Salmon Balls 47

Cod and Mushrooms Mix 48

Creamy Sea Bass Mix 48

Dessert and Smothie 49

Tropical Popsicles 49

Mango & Kale Smoothie 49

Fancy Cold Soup Smoothie 49

Almond Butter Chocolate Cups 50

Vanilla Cookies with Chocolate Chips 50

Mango, Cucumber and Spinach Smoothie 51

Apple Muesli 51

Carrot Cake 52

Lemony Steamed Asparagus 52

Spiced Tea Pudding 52

Fresh Peach Smoothie 53

Other wonderful recipes 53

Mushroom Squash with Vegetable Soup 53

Baked Navy Beans 54

Honey Mustard Chicken 55

Cheddar & Kale Frittata 55

Cabbage Soup 56

Chicken with Snow Peas and Brown Rice 56

Beef and Mushroom Pasta 57

Tabbouleh Salad 57

White Bean Chicken with Winter Green Vegetables 58

Rosemary and Garlic Sweet Potatoes 58

Recipe	Page
Breakfast Burgers with Avocado Buns	59
Shrimp Pasta with Lemon and Garlic	59
Sweet Potato Chips	60
Strawberry Granita	60
Ruby Pears Delight	61
Pasta Primavera	61
Tricky Cheesy Yellow Sauce	62
Fresh Tuna Steak and Fennel Salad	62
Healthy Red Cabbage	63
Easy Chicken and Broccoli	63
Sweet Potato and Butternut Squash Curry	63
Romesco Sauce with Vegetables and Sheet Pan Chicken	64
Zuppa Toscana	65
Healthy Broccoli Soup	65
Shrimp and Mango Mix	66
Lemon-Herb Tilapia	66
Ginger-Broccoli Salad	66
Oregano Dressing on Salad Greens	67
Chocolate-Coated Banana	67
Refreshing Apple Smoothie	68
Delicious Mango Smoothie	68
Healthy Spinach Smoothie	69
Full Coconut Cake	69
Blueberry Crisp	69
Vanilla Coconut Cake	70
Chocolate Bananas	70
Sweet Porridge Dessert	71
Mini Spinach Muffins	71
Lemon Ginger Broccoli and Carrots	72
A simple pudding sweetened with peanut butter	73
Rice Pudding	73
Quick Fish Bowl	73
Quinoa Salmon Bowl	74
Manhattan-Style Salmon Chowder	74
Almond & Chia Bites with Cherries	75

Impressive Parfait with Yogurt, Berry, And Walnut..................................75
Quinoa & Spinach Salad..................................76
Winter Style Fruit Salad..................................76
Limey Cilantro with Shrimp Salad..................................76
Snow Pea and Watermelon Salad..................................77

40 Day Meal Plan..................................78

INTRODUCTION: WHAT IS THE DEFINITION OF INFLAMMATION?

It is vital to have a strategy when making any type of lifestyle change. Particularly when it comes to food, not having a plan might leave you disappointed and broke. Changing your diet has an impact on several aspects of your life.

If you don't live alone, you will also need to consider your family's nutritional demands, preferences, allergies, finances, and time availability. You'll also need to determine which foods to include and which to exclude from your anti-inflammatory diet. You may effectively create a strategy that clears your route to lower inflammation by incorporating all of this knowledge. Both the synergistic effects of foods ingested in combination and those derived from individual foods contribute to the anti-inflammatory benefits. A person's health can be significantly improved by making even little dietary modifications. Therefore, it's crucial to concentrate on your own goals and make them as attainable as you can.

For instance, adding more fruits or legumes to one's breakfast or lunch might help someone make long-lasting dietary adjustments that will improve their general health and reduce inflammation. However, your diet may need to be changed, as well as the kinds of anti-inflammatory items you should eat, depending on your prior medical history. Before starting this adventure, it would be a good idea to see a dietician.

Since this diet is quite simple, I genuinely believe that starting it doesn't require much contemplation. Simply choose nutritious foods and look for recipes you might like since, just like with any diet, if you don't like it, you won't stick with it for very long. Please bear in mind that perfection is not asked of you. Kiss it and take it gently. By which I mean Keep It Stupid Simple. If you're at a friend's wedding, kindly eat a piece of cake unless you are subject to any kind of medically restricted diet restrictions. Life is too precious to waste; it should be appreciated.

WHY THE ANTI-INFLAMMATORY DIET HELPS THE IMMUNE SYSTEM

Inflammation is a part of the immune system's reaction to infection or damage. It's the body's method of notifying the immune system that damaged tissues need to be repaired and that germs and viruses must be protected. Infections may quickly spread inside the body without inflammation. Every day, the body experiences acute inflammation from a sore throat or sprained ankle. These are short-term responses that their body experiences to localize the injury or infection. Acute inflammation causes the blood vessels in the afflicted part of the body to enlarge and increase blood flow. White blood cells are the initial line of defense that reach the inflamed region. The infection is contained by white blood cells, which attract other immune system cells. The affected area gets red and swollen in addition to being red since there is so much going on. Inflammation is a process acting as a natural immune response that keeps us alive and healthy. There are two types of inflammation: acute and chronic. Acute inflammation is characterized by a single bout of swelling and discomfort that subsides when the damage heals. Chronic inflammation is a more dangerous disorder that can harm the body's cells and tissues. The hyperactive immune system, which produces cytokines, is the most well-known cause of chronic inflammation. Cytokines are potent molecules that have been related to almost every human illness. Inflammation is the root of many diseases and ailments. Any ailment that ends in "itis" has inflammation: arthritis, endocarditis, appendicitis, bronchitis, colitis, and laryngitis, to name a few. Everyone is affected by inflammation, but those with weakened immune systems, such as children, the elderly, and those with chronic illnesses, are more vulnerable. Fast food items include hamburgers, hotcakes, French fries, and cookies. Processed meats such as canned meats, luncheon meat, bacon, sausages, and bacon products Added sugars, which are included in a variety of sweets, including ice cream, cakes, and doughnuts, and go by a variety of names Sweet beverages, such as sugary sodas and pressed fruit juices. Check the food value labels for the following names:

Dextrose, maltose, fructose, honey, table sugar, corn syrup, and honey (and the list goes on)

Seed oils are used in the industry. Heavy refinement in mass-produced seed oils has been linked to increased free radicals and inflammation (Fritsch, 2014). These contain many omega6 fatty acids, which in large doses can harm cells and create inflammation.

- Oil from soy
- Canola oil with rapeseed oil
- Oil from corn
- Olive oil

Trans fats are referred to as hydrogenated oils (seed oils that undergo a chemical change to appear in a solid form at room temperature)

Excessive alcohol intake interacts with your gut microbiota and results in an imbalance that causes inflammatory problems. Refined carbohydrates are foods manufactured from white flour, such as white pasta, white bread, noodles, and white rice. Eat No inflammatory Foods. Anything that is highly processed, excessively fatty, or too sugary should be avoided if you have inflammation. Sweets, cakes, cookies, and soda all lead to weight gain, high blood sugar, and high cholesterol (all of which are associated with inflammation) since they are convenient and low in nutrition. Your body's cytokines, which are inflammatory signals, are released in response to sugar. Soda and other sugary drinks are the main offenders. Experts on anti-inflammatory diets generally advise against consuming additional sugars, such as agave and honey. High fat and processed red meat: If taken in excess, these foods might cause inflammation since they are high in saturated fat.

Saturated fat is now again a problem in foods like butter, whole milk, and cheese.

Instead, eat low-fat dairy products. They don't appear to be provocative.

This is because maize oil, safflower oil, and other vegetable oils contain omega6 fatty acids. Naturally, having some omega6 fatty acids would be beneficial, but consuming too much might disturb your body's delicate balance of omega6 and omega3 fatty acids, increasing inflammation.

Margarine, coffee creamers, and other products containing trans fats: Trans fats raise LDL cholesterol and cause inflammation (look for "partially hydrogenated oils" on the label). There is no safe quantity to eat or drink, so refrain.

For barley, rye, and wheat the subject at hand is controversial: gluten. People with celiac disease need to stay away from gluten. The evidence is clear. Nevertheless, whole grains are suitable for the rest of us.

WHAT ARE THE CONSEQUENCES OF CHRONIC INFLAMMATION?

When your body is in a condition of chronic inflammation for a long time, it starts to pain. Simply put, what was supposed to save and protect your body from harm now has the opposite effect. As a result, long-term chronic inflammation will cause significant damage to your healthy cells, organs, and tissues. Long-term inflammatory issues are linked to tissue death and DNA damage, as well as the formation of scar tissue, which can be uncomfortable over time.

Acute inflammation, in particular, is a quick reaction to injury or illness. It's also frequently contained in a small region. When it comes to inflammation, there are five cardinal indications to look for: (1) pain, (2) redness, (3) heat, (4) swelling, and (5) loss of function. Inflammation symptoms commonly appear within the first few hours and days after an illness or injury.

While these symptoms may indicate the presence of inflammation, appropriate testing is required to identify inflammation. A medical practitioner must conduct a thorough medical history and physical examination.

In addition, the medical professional must assess for other symptoms, X-rays, and blood testing. According to studies, chronic inflammation has been related to a range of diseases.

Diabetes, heart disease, Alzheimer's disease, and cancer are all considered inflammatory disorders.

The following are some of the diseases linked to inflammation: Heart Disease: Chronic inflammation is a long-term illness that causes plaque to build in the arteries, resulting in heart attacks and strokes. Inflammation may be triggered by a number of factors, the most common of which is poor eating habits. Inflammation can be caused by a variety of factors, including:

Diet: One of the most prevalent causes of inflammation is poor diet.

Animal products, refined carbs such as dairy, red meat, fried meals, refined sugar, baked goods, and highly processed foods are all unhealthy. These meals are connected to saturated or Tran's fat, which causes our bodies to become more inflamed.

Stress: Cortisol chemicals are produced in your body due to stress. These hormones are produced by two adrenal glands. As a result, when you're stressed, your cortisol levels rise. Your immune cells lose their sensitivity as a result of this, which is one of the reasons for inflammation.

Aging: Aging is a normal process in which our body cells replenish, but some cells begin to die. One of the reasons for inflammation is the trash created during this procedure. Aging is an inflammatory process that leads to age-related diseases. Alzheimer's disease, type 2 diabetes, cancer, and cardiovascular disease are all diseases that affect the brain.

Sleep disorders: An irregular and poor sleeping pattern have been associated with infection development. As a result of the illness, the sleeping cycle is disrupted, and inflammation rises. Sleep difficulties are linked to the most significant diseases and health issues, such as diabetes, high blood pressure, heart attack, and so on.

Obesity: Obesity is linked to inflammation, and gaining weight increases inflammation. Increased inflammation is caused by excess fatty tissue. One of the most efficient strategies to decrease inflammation is to lose weight.

Smoking: One of the high-risk factors for various chronic illnesses is smoking. Tobacco usage can lower your body's ability and diminish the generation of white blood cells. As a result, long-term chronic inflammation is one of the primary causes of DNA damage, raising the risk of colon cancer.

Other consequences can be:
- Type 2 diabetes
- Cardiac ailments
- Cancers
- Rheumatoid arthritis
- Asthma
- Neurodegenerative diseases, including dementia
- Inflammatory bowel disease

WHAT EXACTLY IS AN ANTI-INFLAMMATORY DIET?

The types of food you eat will play a huge role in managing or even avoiding inflammation. Some foods are classified as anti-inflammatory substances and will help fight inflammation. Such food will be high in the following commodities:

Polyphenols Antioxidants Omega3 essential oils Fiber

Eating well isn't as difficult as you might think. Along with all of the "convenient" ready-to-eat unhealthy meals, there are items that may be combined to make a quick and nutritious dinner.

Foods That Can Help You Fight Inflammation

Several foods can reduce inflammation. They provide an alternative to pharmaceuticals; hence, adopting an anti-inflammatory diet will benefit your general health. The most excellent method to improve your happiness, mental wellbeing, and cognitive health is to eat a balance of healthy grains, complex carbohydrates, and fresh veggies. These are the fundamental considerations in developing the dishes in The Anti-inflammatory Diet Cookbook. The following food kinds should ideally be included in your pantry:

- Organic/fresh vegetables
- Collard greens, kale, and spinach
- Broccoli, tomatoes, carrots, peppers, cauliflower
- Sweet potatoes
- Artichokes
- Beans, such as kidney beans, red beans, black beans, and pinto beans
- Healthy fats
- Avocados
- Coconuts
- Olive oil
- Nut butter (almond, hazelnut, coconut)
- Grass-fed meat
- Fatty fish, such as tuna, mackerel, and salmon. Try to choose wild-caught fish, and not the farmed variety, if possible
- Free-range, pastured, and organic eggs
- Nuts, like almonds, pistachios, walnuts, and pecans
- Fruits, like cherries, grapes, oranges, apples, blackberries, strawberries, and raspberries
- Lentils and pulses for protein

Anti-inflammatory qualities are abundant in many household components. One of the most natural and efficient ways to decrease inflammation is to use home remedies. One of the most effective strategies to combat these diseases is to eat an anti-inflammatory diet. Natural anti-inflammatories can be found in the following kitchen items.

Turmeric: Turmeric is a beautiful spice that can be found in almost any kitchen and has therapeutic benefits. It has been used for ages to cure infections, wounds, liver illness, and the common cold as one of the most refined anti-inflammatory foods. Curcumin is one of the turmeric chemicals that helps decrease inflammation, according to research and studies. Ginger: Ginger has long been used as a traditional medicine to treat various ailments, including nausea, headaches, and infections. It's available in the market as a powder or raw root. It helps relieve muscular discomfort and is particularly useful for arthritis because of its anti-inflammatory effects.

Garlic: Garlic has a strong flavor and is antibacterial and anti-inflammatory in nature. Garlic is beneficial to your health as well as adds taste to your diet. Garlic is one of the recognized anti-inflammatory compounds that can help with arthritic symptoms, according to the study. Clove: Another spice with a strong perfume is clove. It's easy to find in any kitchen. Antibacterial and anti-inflammatory effects are found in cloves. It also has therapeutic characteristics and has been used to heal oral problems for millennia. It also helps manage blood sugar levels in those with type 2 diabetes. To enhance the flavor of your cuisine, you may use it whole or in powder form.

Black pepper: The king of spices, black pepper is high in antioxidants, anti-inflammatory, and antibacterial qualities. According to the study and research, black peppers, which contain a lot of the chemical piperine, are helpful when acute inflammation is still in its early stages.

BREAKFASTS

Walnut and Banana Bowl

Prep Time: 13minutes **Total Time:** 30minutes **Yield:** 4

Ingredients:
2 c. water
1 c. steel cut oats
1 c. almond milk
1 tsp. vanilla flavoring
¼ c. walnuts,
2 tbsps. chia chopped seeds
2 bananas

Directions:
Toss all ingredients in a pot. Cook on simmer over medium high heat for about 15minutes. Serve and enjoy!

NUTRITION: Calories: 162 Fat: 4g Carbohydrates: 11g Protein: 4g

Sweet Potato Oat Bars

Servings: 6 **Cooking Time:** 35 Minutes

Ingredients:
Sweet potato, cooked, mashed
1 cup Almond milk, unsweetened
0.75 cups of Egg
1 Date paste
5 tablespoons Vanilla extract
5 teaspoons Baking soda

1 teaspoon Cinnamon, ground
1 teaspoon Cloves, ground
0.25 teaspoon Nutmeg, ground
0.5 teaspoon Ginger, ground
0.5 teaspoon Flaxseed, ground
2 tablespoons Protein powder
1 serving Coconut flour
0.25 cup Oat flour
1 cup Dried coconut, unsweetened
0.25 cup Pecans, chopped
0.25 cup

Directions:
Warm the oven to Fahrenheit 375 degrees and line a square eightbyeight inch baking dish with kitchen parchment. You want to leave some parchment paper hanging over the sides of the pan for lifting once the bars are done baking.
Into your stand blender, add all of the ingredients for the sweet potato oat bars except for the dried coconut and chopped pecans. Allow the mixture to pulse for a few moments until the mixture is smooth and then stop the blender. You may need
to scrape the sides of the blender down and then blend again.
Pour the coconut and pecans into the batter and then stir them in with a spatula.
Do not blend the mixture again, as you don't want these pieces blended. Pour the sweet potato oat bar mixture into your prepared pan and spread it out.
Place your sweet potato oat bar dish in the middle of your oven and allow it to bake until the bars are set through, about twentytwo to twentyfive minutes.
Remove the pan from the oven. Set a wire cooling rack next to the baking dish and then gently lift the kitchen parchment by the overhang and carefully lift it from the dish and onto the wire rack to cool. Allow the sweet potato oat bars to cool completely before slicing.

NUTRITION: Calories: 248 Cal Fat: 14 g Fiber: 4 g Carbs: 10 g Protein: 14 g

Baked Eggs with Portobello Mushrooms

Preparation Time: 8 minutes   **Cooking Time:** 20 minutes   **Servings:** 4

Ingredients:
4 portobello mushroom caps
1 cup arugula
1 medium tomato, chopped
4 large eggs, pasture-raised
salt and pepper to taste

Directions:
Preheat the oven to 3500F and line a baking sheet with parchment paper.
Scoop out the gills from the mushrooms using a spoon. Discard the gills and set aside.
Place the mushrooms on the baking sheet inverted (gill side up) and fill each cap with arugula and tomato.
Carefully crack an egg on each mushroom cap.

Bake in the oven for 20 minutes or until the eggs have set.

NUTRITION: Calories: 80 Total Fat: 5g Saturated Fat: 2g Total Carbs: 5g Net Carbs: 3g Protein: 5g Sugar: 3g

Milk and Creamy Yogurt Bowl
Prep Time: 10 minutes **Cook time:** 10 minutes **Serves** 1

Ingredients:
1 tablespoon heavy whipping cream
½ cup plain whole milk Greek yogurt
1 tablespoon unsweetened pumpkin puree
1 teaspoon pumpkin pie spice (no sugar added)
1 to 2 teaspoons monk fruit extract or sugarfree sweetener (optional) ½ teaspoon vanilla extract
2 tablespoons coarsely chopped pecans

Directions:
In a small bowl, using an immersion blender or whisk, whisk the cream for 2 to 3 minutes, until thick and doubled in volume. Set aside.
In a medium bowl, mix together the yogurt, pumpkin, pumpkin pie spice, sweetener (if using), and vanilla.
Top the yogurt mixture with the pecans and whipped cream and serve.

NUTRITION: Calories: 266 Fat:20g Protein: 13g Total Carbs: 9g Fiber: 2g Net Carbs: 7g

A Quick antipasto pasta
Prep Time: 10 minutes **Cooking Time**: 15 minutes **Servings**: 1

Ingredients:
300g farfalle pasta
1/3 cup basil leaves
1/4 cup (40g) pine nuts, toasted
1/4 cup (20g) finely grated parmesan
1 garlic clove, crushed
120g pkt Coles Australian Baby Rocket
1/2 cup (125ml) olive oil
100g thickly sliced Don Ham on the Bone from the Deli, torn 50g slices Coles Deli Herb Coated Salami, chopped
100g Coles Danish Fetta, coarsely crumbled
140g Coles Deli Giant Pitted Kalamata Olives, halved
170g Coles Deli Semi Dried Tomatoes with Fresh Basil, coarsely chopped

Directions:
Cook the pasta in a large pot of boiling water according to the package recommendations, or until al dente. Drain well, saving 12 cups (125ml)
of the cooking liquid. Then, reintroduce the farfalle pasta to the pan.
Meanwhile, combine the basil, pine nuts, parmesan, garlic, and half of the rocket in a food processor and process until finely chopped. While the engine is running, pour the oil in a thin, steady stream until well blended. Season.

Combine the pesto, ham, salami, feta, olive, tomato, leftover cooking liquid, and remaining rocket in the pan with the farfalle pasta. Toss gently to blend. Distribute the pasta mixture among the serving dishes. Serve right away.

Orange Oatmeal Muffins

Prep Time: 7 minutes.   **Cook time**: 15 minutes.   **Serves**: 6

Ingredients:
3 cups old fashioned rolled oats
1 teaspoon baking powder
¼ teaspoon salt
1 teaspoon ground cinnamon
¼ cup vanilla almond milk, unsweetened
¼ cup fresh orange juice
3 ⅓ cups mashed bananas
1 large egg
¼ cup erythritol

Directions:
In a suitable bowl, mix all of the ingredients together, while stirring until well combined.
Place six silicone muffin cups inside of a 6" cake pan. Spoon the oatmeal mixture into the muffin cups. Cover this pan with aluminium foil.
Pour 1 cup water into the insert of the Instant Pot and set the steam rack inside. Set the cake pan with the muffins on the rack. Close the lid and secure it well.
Pressure cook for 15 minutes.
When cooked, release the pressure quickly until the float valve drops and then unlock lid.
Carefully remove this pan from the insert of the Instant pot and remove the foil from the top. Let the muffins cool 15 minutes before eating. They will become firmer as they cool.

NUTRITION: Calories 148; Fat 5g; Sodium 117mg; Carbs 29g; Fiber 8g; Sugars 5g; Protein 5g

Coconut Rice with Berries

Prep Time: 10 minutes.   **Cooking time**: 30 minutes.   **Servings**: 2

Ingredients:
¾ cup water
¾ teaspoon salt
½ cup fresh blueberries, or raspberries, divided ½ cup shaved coconut, divided
½ cup brown basmati rice
½ cup coconut milk
2 pitted and chopped dates
¼ cup toasted slivered almonds, divided

Directions:
Combine the water, basmati rice, coconut milk, spice, and date pieces in a medium saucepan over high heat.
Stir constantly until the mixture boils. Set the heat to low and cook, occasionally stirring, for 20 to 30 minutes, or until the rice is tender.
Place some blueberries, almonds, and coconut on top of each serving of rice.

Blueberry Breakfast Blend

Prep Time: 8 minutes. **Cooking time**: 0 minutes. **Servings**: 1

Ingredients:
¹/₃ teaspoon turmeric
½ cup spinach
¾ cup fresh blueberries
1 cup fresh pineapple chunks
1 cup water
1 tablespoon chia seeds
1 tablespoon lemon juice

Directions:
Combine all the ingredients in your blender. Blend to a smooth consistency.

NUTRITION: Calories: 260 Fat: 6 g Protein: 13 g Sodium: 30 mg Total carbs: 35 g

Golden Milk

Prep Time: 5 Minutes **Cooking Time**: 5 Minutes **Servings**: 2

Ingredients:
1 tbsp. Coconut Oil
1 ½ cups Coconut Milk, light
Pinch of Pepper
1 ½ cups Almond Milk, unsweetened
¼ tsp. Ginger, grated
1 ½ tsp. Turmeric, grounded
¼ tsp. Cinnamon, grounded
Sweetener of your choice, as needed

Directions:
To make this healthy beverage, you need to place all the ingredients in a mediumsized saucepan and mix it well.
After that, heat it over medium heat for 3 to 4 minutes or until it is hot but not boiling. Stir continuously.
Taste for seasoning. Add more sweetener or spice as required by you.
Finally, transfer the milk to the serving glass and enjoy it.
Tip: Instead of cinnamon powder, you can also use the cinnamon stick, which can be discarded at the end if you prefer a much more intense flavor.

NUTRITION: Calories: 205Kcal Proteins: 2g Carbohydrates: 9g Fat: 15g

Spiced Morning Chia Pudding

Prep Time: 10 Minutes **Cooking Time**: 5 Minutes **Servings**: 1

Ingredients:
½ tsp. Cinnamon
1 ½ cups Cashew Milk
1/8 tsp. Cardamom, grounded

1/3 cup Chia Seeds
1/8 tsp. Cloves, grounded
2 tbsp. Maple Syrup
1 tsp. Turmeric

Directions:
To begin with, combine all the ingredients in a medium bowl until well mixed.
Next, spoon the mixture into a container and allow it to sit overnight.
In the morning, transfer to a cup and serve with toppings of your choice.
Tip: You can top it with toppings of your choice like coconut flakes or seeds etc.

NUTRITION: Calories: 237Kcal Proteins: 1g Carbohydrates: 29g Fat: 1g

Beet and Cherry Smoothie

Prep Time: 5 minutes **Cook time**: 0 minutes **Serves** 4

Ingredients:
10-ounce almond milk, unsweetened
2 small beets, peeled and cut into quarters
½ cup frozen cherries, pitted
½ teaspoon frozen banana
1 tablespoon almond butter

Directions:
Add all ingredients in a blender.
Blend until smooth.

NUTRITION: Calories: 470 Fat: 38g Saturated Fat: 6g Total Carbs: 24g Net Carbs: 14g Protein: 16g Sugar: 10g

Breakfast and Brunch Mushroom Crepes

Servings: 4 **Cooking Time**: 25 Minutes

Ingredients:
1 cup wholewheat flour
1 tsp onion powder
½ tsp baking soda
¼ tsp sea salt
1 cup crumbled tofu
⅓ cup almond milk
¼ cup lemon juice
2 tbsp extravirgin olive oil
½ cup chopped mushrooms
½ cup finely chopped onion
2 cups collard greens

Directions:
Combine the flour, onion powder, baking soda, and salt in a bowl.
Place the tofu, almond milk, lemon juice, and oil in your food processor. Blitz until everything is well combined. Add to the the flour mixture and mix to combine. Stir in mushrooms, onion, and collard greens.
Heat a skillet and grease with cooking spray. Lower the heat and spread a ladleful of the batter across the surface of the skillet. Cook for 4 minutes on both sides or until set. Remove to a plate. Repeat the process until no batter is left, greasing with a little more oil, if needed.
Serve.

NUTRITION: Per Serving: Calories: 282;Fat: 15g;Protein: 10g;Carbs: 30g.

Fruit and Millet Breakfast

Prep Time: 30 minutes **Cooking time**: 15 minutes **Servings**: 2

Millet is a super grain full of nutrients and, when combined with fruits, makes a wholesome breakfast for anyone.

Ingredients:
½ C. millet
1 C. water
2 tbsp. raisins
1 tbsp. currants
⅛ tsp. cinnamon
⅛ tsp. vanilla extract
1 C. coconut milk, unsweetened and divided
1 tsp. honey
½ C. raspberries
½ C. blueberries
1 tsp. hemp hearts
1 tsp. chia seeds
1 tsp. mint, chopped

Directions:
Place millet and water in a medium saucepan over medium heat.
Bring to a boil, and then add the raisins, currants, cinnamon, and vanilla.
Cover with a lid, reduce heat to low, and let it cook for another 10
minutes until liquid is absorbed.
Turn heat off and let sit for 11 minutes.
Add coconut milk, honey, raspberries, blueberries, hemp hearts, and chia seeds. Turn heat to low and let cook for 2 minutes.
Transfer to bowls and garnish with mint.

NUTRITION: Calories: 565 kcal Carbs: 64 g Protein: 10 g Fat: 35 g Fiber: 98

Healthy Chia Pudding

Prep Time: 10 minutes **Cooking Time**: 5 minutes **Serve**: 2

Ingredients:
6 tbsp chia seeds

1 tbsp maple syrup
¼ tsp ground ginger
¼ tsp ground cinnamon
1 ¼ tsp turmeric
2 cups can coconut milk
1/8 tsp ground black pepper

Directions:
Add milk, turmeric, cinnamon, cardamom, ginger, maple syrup, and black pepper into the glass jar and stir until well combined.
Add chia seeds and stir well. Cover jar with lid and place in the fridge for overnight.
Stir well and serve.

NUTRITION:
Calories 892 Fat 75 g Carbohydrates 50.4 g Sugar 6 g Protein 18 g Cholesterol 0 mg

Breakfast Porridge

Prep Time: 10 minutes **Cooking time**: 50 minutes **Servings**: 2

If you like eating something heavy in the mornings, this is for you. It is light but filling, and packed with essential macronutrients for the day.

Ingredients:
½ C. red or wild rice
½ C. steelcut oats
¼ C. pearl barley
1 cinnamon stick
1-2 tbsp. Splenda
¼ tsp. salt
¼ C. fruit, dried (cranberries, cherries, raisins) Nuts, chopped, maple syrup and/or milk, for serving (optional)

Directions:
Soak rice, barley, farina, and oats in 5 C. of water in a rice cooker.
Add cinnamon stick, Splenda, salt, and dried fruit.
Cover the cooker and cook for 50 minutes on 'manual' function.
Serve with nuts on top as desired.

NUTRITION: Calories: 4037 kcal Total Fat: 19 g Saturated Fat: 0.32 g Cholesterol: 0 mg Sodium: 328 mg Carbohydrates: 893 g Fiber: 14 g Sugar: 52 g Protein: 3 g

Lunch

Lemongrass and Ginger Mackerel

Prep Time: 10 minutes **Cooking Time**: 25 minutes **Servings**: 4

Ingredients:
4 mackerel fillets, skinless and boneless
2 tablespoons olive oil
1 tablespoon ginger, grated
2 lemongrass sticks, chopped
2 red chilies, chopped
Juice of 1 lime
A handful parsley, chopped

Directions:
In a roasting pan, combine the mackerel with the oil, ginger and the other ingredients, toss and bake at 390 degrees F for 25 minutes.
Divide everything between plates and serve.

NUTRITION: Calories: 251Fat: 3Fiber: 4Carbs: 14

Brown Rice and Shitake Miso Soup with Scallions
Servings: 4 Cooking Time: 45 Minutes

Ingredients:
2 tablespoons sesame oil
1 cup thinly sliced shiitake mushroom caps
1 garlic clove, minced
1 (1½inch) piece fresh ginger, peeled and sliced
1 cup mediumgrain brown rice
½ teaspoon salt
1 tablespoon white miso
2 scallions, thinly sliced
2 tablespoons finely chopped fresh cilantro

Directions:
Heatup the oil over mediumhigh heat in a large pot.
Add the mushrooms, garlic, and ginger and sauté until the mushrooms begin to soften about 5 minutes.
Put the rice and stir to coat with the oil evenly. Add 2 cups of water and salt and boil.
Simmer within 30 to 40 minutes. Use a little of the soup broth to soften the miso, then stir it into the pot until well blended.
Mix in the scallions plus cilantro, then serve.

NUTRITION: Calories 265 Total Fat: 8g Total Carbohydrates: 43g Sugar: 2g Fiber: 3g Protein: 5g Sodium: 456mg

Capellini Soup with Tofu And Shrimp
Servings: 8 Cooking Time: 20 Mins

Ingredients:
4 cups of bok choy, sliced
1/4pound shrimp, peeled, deveined
1 block firm tofu, sliced into squares
1 can sliced water chestnuts, drained

1 bunch scallions, sliced
2 cups reducedsodium chicken broth
2 teaspoons soy sauce, reducedsodium
2 cups capellini
2 teaspoons of sesame oil
Freshly ground white pepper
1 teaspoon of rice wine vinegar

Directions:
Pour the broth in a saucepan over mediumhigh heat. Bring to a boil. Add the shrimp, bok choy, oil, and sauce. Allow to boil and turn the heat to low. Simmer for 5 minutes.
Add the water chestnuts, pepper, vinegar, tofu, capellini, and scallions. Cook for 5 minutes or until the capellini is barely tender. Serve while hot.

NUTRITION: Calories 205 carbs: 20g fat: 9g protein: 9g

Chicken and Brussels sprouts

Prep Time: 10 minutes **Cooking Time**: 10 minutes **Servings**: 4

Ingredients:
1 cored, peeled and chopped apple
1 chopped yellow onion
1 tbsp. organic olive oil
3 c. shredded Brussels sprouts
1 lb. ground chicken meat
Black pepper

Directions:
Heat up a pan while using oil over mediumhigh heat, add chicken, stir and brown for 5 minutes.
Add Brussels sprouts, onion, black pepper and apple, stir, cook for 10 minutes, divide into bowls and serve.
1. Enjoy!

NUTRITION: Calories: 200Fat: 8 g Carbs: 13 g Protein: 9 g Sugars: 3 g Sodium: 194 mg

Bean Shawarma Salad

Servings: 2 **Cooking Time**: 20 Minutes

Ingredients:
For Preparing Salad
20 Pita chips
5ounces Spring lettuce
10 Cherry tomatoes
¾ Cup fresh parsley
¼ Cup red onion (chop)
For Chickpeas
1tablespoon Olive oil
1 Headingtablespoon cumin and turmeric
½ Headingtablespoon paprika and coriander powder

1 Pinch black pepper
½ Scant Kosher salt
¼ tablespoon Ginger and cinnamon powder For Preparing Dressing
3 Garlic Cloves
1 tablespoon Dried drill
1 tablespoon Lime juice Water
½ Cup hummus

Directions:
Place a rack in the already preheated oven (204C). Mix chickpeas with all spices and herbs.
Place a thin layer of chickpeas on the baking sheet and bake it almost for 20
minutes. Bake it until the beans are golden brown.
For preparing the dressing, mix all ingredients in a whisking bowl and blend it.
Add water gradually for appropriate smoothness.
Mix all herbs and spices for preparing salad.
For serving, add pita chips and beans in the salad and drizzle some dressing over it.

NUTRITION: Calories 173 Carbs: 8g Fat: 6g Protein: 19g

Cod and Quinoa Mix

Prep Time: 10 minutes **Cooking Time**: 25 minutes **Servings**: 4

Ingredients
3 scallions, chopped
2 cups chicken stock
1 pound cod fillets, boneless and cubed
1 cup black quinoa
2 tablespoons olive oil
2 celery stalks, chopped
A pinch of salt and black pepper
1 tablespoon coriander, chopped

Directions:
Heat up a pan with the oil over mediumhigh heat, add the scallions and the celery and sauté for 5 minutes.
Add the fish and cook for 5 minutes more.
Add the rest of the ingredients, toss, cook over medium heat for 15
minutes more, divide everything between plates and serve.
NUTRITION: Calories: 261Fat: 4Fiber: 6Carbs: 14Protein: 7

Jicama Black Bean Salad

Prep Time: 10 minutes. **Cook time**: 50 minutes. **Serves**: 4

Ingredients:
1 cup mediumor longgrain brown rice
5 tablespoons extravirgin olive oil
2 teaspoons salt
1 (15ounce) can black beans, drained and rinsed 1 small jicama, peeled and cut into ¼ inch dice ¼ cup chopped fresh cilantro

¼ cup lime juice, freshly squeezed
2 scallions, both white and green parts, sliced 1 small jalapeño pepper, seeded and minced
¼ teaspoon black pepper, freshly ground

Directions:
In a suitable pot, combine the rice, 2 cups of water, 1 tablespoon of oil, and 1
teaspoon of salt. Bring to a boil, Reduce its heat to a simmer, cover, and cook until the rice is tender, 40 to 45 minutes. Remove from the heat, let cool to room temperature, and fluff with a fork.
Add the beans, jicama, cilantro, lime juice, scallions, jalapeño pepper, remaining 4 tablespoons of oil, remaining 1 teaspoon of salt, and the pepper, and mix well. Serve at room temperature, or chill for several hours to serve cold.

NUTRITION: Calories 384; Fat 19g; Sodium 782mg; Carbs 57g; Fiber 14g; Sugars 7g; Protein 12g

Cherry-balsamic Chicken Breasts

Servings: 4 **Cooking Time**: 40 Minutes

Ingredients:
2 tbsp parsley, chopped
4 chicken breasts
2 scallions, sliced
2 tbsp coconut oil
¾ cup chicken broth
1 tbsp balsamic vinegar
½ cup dried cherries
Sea salt and pepper to taste

Directions:
Preheat your oven to 375ºF. Melt the coconut oil in a large skillet over medium heat. Season the chicken with salt and pepper. Place the chicken in the pan and brown it on both sides, 3 minutes per side. Add the scallions, chicken broth, balsamic vinegar, and dried cherries.
Cover with an ovenproof lid or aluminum foil and place the pan in the preheated oven. Bake for 20 minutes, or until the chicken is cooked through. Top with parsley.

NUTRITION: Per Serving: Calories: 380;Fat: 15g;Protein: 42g;Carbs: 17g.

Creamy Turkey with Mushrooms

Servings: 4 **Cooking Time**: 40 Minutes

Ingredients:
1 ½ lb turkey breasts, boneless and skinless 6 oz white button mushrooms, sliced
3 tbsp chopped shallots
½ tsp dried thyme
½ cup dry white wine
1 cup chicken stock
1 garlic clove, minced
2 tbsp olive oil
3 tbsp coconut cream
1 ½ tbsp arrowroot

Sea salt and pepper to taste

Directions:
Tie the turkey breast with a kitchen string horizontally, leaving approximately 2 inches apart. Season with salt and pepper. Heat half of the olive oil in your Instant Pot on "Sauté". Add the turkey and brown it for 3 minutes on each side. Transfer to a plate. Add the remaining oil, followed by the shallots, thyme, garlic, and mushrooms and cook for 5 minutes or until translucent. Add white wine and scrape up the brown bits from the bottom.

When the alcohol evaporates, return the turkey to the pot. Add the broth. Close the lid and cook for 20 minutes on "Manual". Combine the coconut cream and arrowroot in a bowl. Stir in the pot. Bring the sauce to a boil, then turn the cooker off. Slice the turkey in half and serve topped with the creamy mushroom sauce.

NUTRITION: Calories: 192;Fat: 5g;Protein: 15g;Carbs: 12g.

Shirataki Pasta with Avocado and Cream

Prep Time: 10minutes   **Total time**: 16   **Yield**: 2servings

Ingredients:
½ packet cooked
½ avocado
shirataki noodles
½ tsp. black pepper,
½ tsp. salt cracked
½ tsp. basil, dried
1/8 c. cream, heavy

Directions:
In a medium pot, add water until half full. Set over medium heat and allow to boil. Add in noodles and let cook for about 2minutes. Drain noodles and place them aside. Add avocado to a bowl and mash using a fork. Set in a blender alongside the other ingredients. Process well to get a smooth consistency. Set your heat to medium. Add noodles and avocado, mix in a frying pan and cook over heat for 2minutes. Serve.

NUTRITION: Calories 131 Total Fat 16g Total Carbs 9g Protein 2g Sugar 0.3g

Energy Bites

Prep time: 20 minutes   **Cook time:** 0 minutes   **Servings:** 24

Ingredients:
½ cup sunflower seeds
¼ cup pumpkin seeds
20 medium whole dates, pitted and chopped
¾ cup shredded coconut
½ cup cacao powder
2 tablespoons coconut oil
⅛ teaspoon salt
1 ½ tablespoons water

Directions:

Put seeds in a food processor and pulse until they are chopped (but not super fine like a powder).
Add dates, ½ cup shredded coconut, ¼ cup cacao, oil, salt, and water and process until ingredients are well mixed and mixture looks uniform.
Using a tablespoon, spoon out mixture and roll into balls.
Put the remaining ¼ cup shredded coconut and ¼ cup cacao on two separate flat plates. Coat balls with cacao or coconut by rolling half of balls in one, and half in the other. Place completed balls on a parchment paper–lined baking sheet.
Refrigerate at least 30 minutes (or up to overnight) until they harden. They will keep in refrigerator in an airtight container or plastic bag up to 2 weeks.

NUTRITION: Calories 56; Fat 3.51g; Sodium 25mg; Carbs 6.53g; Fiber 3g; Sugars 4.07g; Protein 1.5g

Banana Pops

Prep time: 15 minutes **Cook time:** 0 minutes **Servings:** 4

Ingredients:
¼ cup dark chocolate chips (cacao or higher) 2 large ripe bananas
4 popsicle sticks
½ cup plain, whole milk Greek yogurt
½ cup antiinflammatory granola, crushed into small chunks Prepare a baking sheet with parchment paper. Be sure tray will fit in a freezer.
Fill a medium saucepan ⅓ of the way with water. Place a suitable bowl on top of it. It should fit securely, but bottom of bowl should not touch bottom of pot. Place chocolate in bowl and melt, while stirring occasionally.
Peel bananas and cut them in half crosswise. Insert sticks into cut ends of bananas.
Place yogurt in a small shallow bowl.
Place granola on a flat plate.
To assemble, dip and roll banana in yogurt. Spread with back of a spoon or pastry brush to make sure it is well coated. Then roll banana in granola until it is evenly coated. Use your fingers to gently help granola stick.
Place banana pops on sheet and drizzle melted chocolate evenly over them.
Place tray in freezer at least 2 hours or up to overnight to firm up toppings.
Serve.

NUTRITION: Calories 179; Fat 11.9g; Sodium 30mg; Carbs 41.9g; Fiber 4.3g; Sugars 23.5g; Protein 7.9g

Almond-Orange Torte

Prep time: 45 minutes **Cook time:** 1 hr. 30 minutes **Servings:** 16

Ingredients:
3 large oranges
2 bay leaves
1 cinnamon stick
¾ cup sucanat
6 large eggs
½ teaspoon baking powder
3 ½ cups almond meal
1 cup hazelnut meal

¾ cup dark chocolate chips (cacao or higher) At 350 degrees F, preheat your oven grease and flour a 9" × 13" pan.

Directions:
In a medium pot, combine oranges, bay leaves, and cinnamon and cover with water. Bring to a boil and simmer over low heat 45 minutes until oranges are easily pierced with a fork. Cut them in quarters and let cool. Take out seeds and blend in a food processor until mash is chunky but even.
In a suitable bowl, combine orange purée, sucanat, eggs, baking powder, and nut meals. Mix well, then fold in chocolate chips.
Pour batter into prepared cake pan. Bake the food for 40–45 minutes.
Let cool at least 30 minutes before serving.

NUTRITION: Calories 220; Fat 16.6g; Sodium 36mg; Carbs 13.4g; Fiber 3.9g; Sugars 7.6g; Protein 8.2g

Raspberry and Chard Smoothie

Prep time: 5 minutes **Cooking time:** 0 minute **Servings:** 2

Chard and raspberry might not be your favorites, but they are rich in antioxidants and curb inflammation.

Ingredients:
2 C. coconut water
2 C. Swiss chards
2 key limes, juiced
2 C. fresh whole raspberries

Directions:
Whizz all the ingredients on high.
Pour into a cup and enjoy.

NUTRITION: Calories: 133.7 kcal Carbohydrates: 31.02 g Fat: 1.47 g Fiber: 12.8 g Protein: 4.2 g

Apple, Berries, and Kale Smoothie

Prep time: 5 minutes **Cooking time:** 0 minute **Servings:** 2

Say goodbye to digestive issues, joint problems and get your daily vitamin C dose in a gulp.

Ingredients:
1 C. spring water
1 C. berries, mixed – blueberries are good
2 C. kale leaves, fresh
1 large apple, cored

Directions:
Whizz all the ingredients on high.
Pour into a cup and enjoy.

NUTRITION: Calories: 119.27 kcal Carbohydrates: 28.55 g Fat: 0.96 g Fiber: 5.3 g Protein: 3.5 g

Orange Banana Alkaline Smoothie

Prep time: 10 minutes **Cooking time:** 0 minutes **Servings:** 2

Ingredients:
½ C. coconut water
1 C. water
2 mediumsize bananas
4 oranges, peeled
¼ tsp. bromide plus powder
2 tsp. lightcolored agave syrup

Directions:
Mash the banana and pour all ingredients into a blender. Blend in 2030 second increments until the mixture is smooth.
Dilute with water to your desired thickness.
Serve in a cup and add some ice cubes or place in a refrigerator.
NUTRITION: Calories: 223.99 kcal Protein: 3.45 g Sugar: 37.84 g Fiber:1.8.14 g

Balsamic Scallops

Prep time: 5 minutes **Cooking Time:** 10 or so minutes **Servings:** 4

Ingredients:
1 pound sea scallops
4 scallions, chopped
2 tablespoons olive oil
1 tablespoon balsamic vinegar
1 tablespoon cilantro, chopped
A pinch of salt and black pepper

Directions:
Heat up a pan with the oil over medium-high heat, add the scallops, the scallions and the other ingredients.
Toss, cook for 10 minutes, divide into bowls and serve.

NUTRITION: Calories: 300   Fat: 4   Fiber: 4   Carbs: 14   Protein: 17

Vegan "Frittata"

Prep Time: 15 minutes **Cooking Time**: 20 minutes **Servings**: 6

Ingredients:
1½ cups garbanzo bean flour
1 teaspoon salt
1 teaspoon ground turmeric
½ teaspoon ground cumin
1 teaspoon chopped fresh sage
1½ cups water
2 tablespoons extravirgin olive oil
1 zucchini, sliced
2 scallions, sliced

Directions:
Preheat the oven to 350°F.
In a medium bowl, whisk together the garbanzo bean flour, salt, turmeric, cumin, and sage.
Slowly add the water, stirring constantly to prevent the batter from getting lumpy. Set aside.
In an ovensafe skillet, heat the oil over high heat. Sauté the zucchini until softened, 2 to 3 minutes. Stir in the scallions, then spoon the batter over the vegetables.
Place the skillet in the oven and bake until firm when jiggled slightly, 20 to 25 minutes.
Serve warm or at room temperature.

NUTRITION: Calories: 140Total Fat: 6gTotal Carbohydrates: 15gSugar: 3gFiber: 3g Protein: 6g Sodium: 410mg

Beets Gazpacho

Prep Time: 10minutes   **Total time**: 20minutes   **Yield**: 4servings

Ingredients:
1× 20oz. Can Great Northern Beans,
¼ tsp. Kosher Salt rinsed and drained
1 tbsp. ExtraVirgin Olive Oil
½ tsp. Garlic, fresh and minced
1× 6oz. pouch Pink Salmon flaked
2 tbsp. Lemon juice, freshly squeezed
4 Green Onions, sliced thinly
½ tsp. Ground Black Pepper
½ tsp. Lemon rind grated
¼ c. Flatleaf Parsley, fresh and chopped

Directions:
First, place lemon rind, olive oil, lemon juice, black pepper, and garlic in a mediumsized mixing bowl and mix them with a whisker. Combine beans, onions, salmon, and parsley in another mediumsized bowl and toss them well. Then, spoon in the lemon juice dressing over the bean's mixture. Mix well ùntil the dressing coats the beans mixture. Serve and enjoy.

NUTRITION: Calories 131, Proteins: 9g Carbohydrates: 18g Fat: 5g

Baked Butternut Squash Rigatoni

Prep Time: 10minutes   **Total time**: 1hour 40minutes   **Yield**: 4servings

Ingredients:
3 clove garlic butternut squash
2 tbsp. olive oil
1 lb. rigatoni
1/2 c. substantial
3 c. destroyed cream fontina
2 tbsp. slashed crisp
1 tbsp. salt sage
1 tsp. naturally,

1 c. panko ground pepper breadcrumbs

Directions:
Preheat broiler to 425 degrees F. In the meantime, in a huge bowl, hurl squash, garlic, and olive oil to cover. Spot on a huge rimmed preparing sheet and dish until delicate, around 60minutes. Set your container on a wire rack
to allow for cooling, around 10minutes. Decrease stove to 350 degrees F. In the meantime, heat a huge pot of salted water to the point of boiling and cook rigatoni as per bundle bearings. Channel and put in a safe spot. Utilizing a blender or nourishment processor, purée held squash with overwhelming cream until smooth. In a huge bowl, hurl squash puree withheld rigatoni, 2
cups fontina, savvy, salt, and pepper. Brush base and sides of a 9by 13inch preparing dish with olive oil. Move rigatonisquash blend to a dish.
In a little bowl, consolidate the remaining fontina and panko. Sprinkle over pasta and heat until brilliant darker, 20 to 25minutes.

NUTRITION: 654kcal , Protein: 343 g, Fat: 492 g, Carbohydrates: 217 g

Anti-inflammatory Chicken Porridge

Prep Time: 10 minutes **Cook time**: 25 minutes **Serves** 2

Ingredients:
¾ cup Almond Milk, unsweetened
2 tbsp. Hemp Seeds
2 tbsp. Chia Seeds, whole
¼ cup Walnuts, halved
¼ cup Almond Butter
¼ cup Coconut Flakes, unsweetened & toasted ¼ cup Coconut Milk
½ tsp. Turmeric Powder
Dash of Black Pepper, grounded, as needed
½ tsp. Cinnamon
1 tbsp. Extra Virgin Olive Oil

Directions:
To start with, heat a large saucepan over medium heat.
To this, put in the hemp seeds, flaked coconut, and chopped walnuts.
Roast for 2 minutes or until toasted.
Once the coconut-seed mixture is roasted, transfer to a bowl and set it aside.
Then, heat almond milk and coconut milk in a wide saucepan over medium heat.
Once it becomes hot but not boiling, remove from the heat. Stir in almond butter and coconut oil to it. Mix.
Now, add chia seeds, pepper powder, turmeric powder, and salt to the milk. Combine.
Keep it aside for 5 minutes and then add half of the roasted coconut mixture. Mix.
Finally, transfer to a serving bowl and top with the remaining coconut mixture.
Serve immediately.

NUTRITION: Calories: 575Kcal   Proteins: 14.8g   Carbohydrates: 6g   Fat: 50.2g

Dinner

Beef, Pork, and Lamb Thai Beef with Coconut Milk

Prep Time: 10 minutes   **Cook time**: 30 minutes   Serves 2

Ingredients:
2 tablespoons coconut oil
1 teaspoon crushed garlic
1 onion cut into wedges
8 ounces (227 g) round steak, cut into strips
2 cups cubed potatoes
1 lime
2 cups cubed Carrots
1 cup coconut milk
½ cup beef stock
Black pepper to taste

Directions:
Heat the wok over a medium heat, and then add in the oil, garlic, and the onion, cooking for 1 minute. Put the beef into the wok and cook for 3
minutes. Add in the potatoes, Carrots into the wok and stirfry for 4
minutes. Add the coconut milk, beef stock, and black pepper and allow to simmer for 20 to 25 minutes or until beef is cooked through. Serve hot with your choice of greens and a wedge of lime to squeeze!

NUTRITION: Calories: 563   fat: 45g   protein: 30g   carbs: 15g   fiber: 3g   sugar: 4g   sodium: 235mg

Berry Bliss Slow Cooker Pork

Prep Time: 10 minutes   **Cook time**: 6 hours   **Serves** 4

Ingredients:
4 thickcut boneless pork chops
1 teaspoon fine Himalayan salt
½ teaspoon ground black pepper
2 tablespoons avocado oil
2 cups raspberries or blackberries
½ cup bone broth
½ cup chopped red onions
¼ cup chopped fresh parsley
¼ cup red wine vinegar
1 teaspoon peeled and minced fresh ginger
Pinch of ground nutmeg
Dash of ground cinnamon
10 drops liquid stevia (optional)

Directions:

Heat a large skillet over medium heat, or heat an electric pressure cooker on sauté mode. Sprinkle the pork chops with the salt and pepper. When the skillet or pressure cooker is hot, pour in the oil and sear the chops for 3
minutes on each side. Place the seared pork chops in the slow cooker so they are all lying flat. Add the remaining ingredients. Cover and cook on low for 6 hours. Remove the lid from the slow cooker and use tongs to carefully remove the pork chops. Serve with the tender berries and sauce spooned on top of the chops. It's quite lovely. Store leftovers in an airtight container in the fridge for up to 4 days. Reheat in a covered skillet over medium heat for 5 to 10 minutes.

NUTRITION: Calories: 432 fat: 14g protein: 44g carbs: 32g fiber: 5g sugar: 26g sodium: 545mg

Fake Mushroom Risotto

Servings: 4 **Cooking Time**: 30 Minutes

Ingredients:
1 ½ head cauliflower
2 cups sliced mushrooms
1 garlic clove, minced
1 tsp dried basil
1 carrot, grated
1 cup vegetable broth
1 tbsp olive oil
½ onion, diced

Directions:
Cut the cauliflower into pieces and place them in your food processor.
Process until really ground (cauliflower rice). You should have about 6 cups of cauliflower rice.
Heat the oil in your Instant Pot set to "Sauté". Sauté the carrots and onions for 3 minutes. Add the garlic and cook for one more minute.
Stir in all of the remaining ingredients. Seal lid and press "Manual"
function. Cook for 5 minutes. Do a quick pressure release. Serve.

NUTRITION: Calories: 120;Fat: 11g;Protein: 3g;Carbs: 14g.

Chicken with Fennel and Zucchini

Prep Time: 15 minutes **Cook time**: 15 minutes **Serves** 4

Ingredients:
2 tablespoons
extravirgin olive oil
4 boneless skinless chicken breasts, cut into strips 1 leek, white part only, sliced thinly
1 fennel bulb, sliced into ¼inch rounds
3 zucchini, sliced into ½inch rounds
½ cup chicken broth
1 teaspoon salt
½ teaspoon freshly ground black pepper
½ cup sliced green olives
2 tablespoons chopped fresh dill

Directions:
In a large pan over high heat, heat the olive oil. Add the chicken strips. Brown them for 1 to 2 minutes, stirring constantly. Transfer the chicken and its juices to a plate or bowl and set aside. Add the leek, fennel, and zucchini to the pan. Sauté for 5 minutes. Return the chicken and juices to the pan. Pour in the broth. Add the salt and pepper. Cover the pan and simmer for 5 minutes. Remove the pan from the heat, and stir in the olives and dill.

NUTRITION: Calories: 418 fat: 20g protein: 45g carbs: 15g Fibre: 4g sugar: 5g sodium: 1021mg

Rosemary Pork Chops

Whether you use fresh or dehydrated rosemary, the benefits are huge and this is delicious.
Prep Time: 30 minutes **Cooking time**: 35 minutes **Servings**: 4

Ingredients
4 pork loin chops, boneless
Salt and black pepper, to taste
4 garlic cloves, minced
1 tbsp. rosemary, chopped
1 tbsp. olive oil

Directions
Combine the pork chops with the rest of the ingredients in a roasting plan, toss, and bake at 425°F for 10 minutes.
Reduce the heat to 350°F and cook the chops for 25 minutes more.
Divide the chops between plates and serve with a side salad.

NUTRITION: Calories: 2678 kcal Fat: 103 g Fiber: 0.2 g Carbs: 26 g Protein: 356 g

Mushroom Risotto

Prep Time: 5 Minutes **Cooking Time**: 25 Minutes **Servings**: 4

Ingredients:
2 Tablespoons Olive Oil
1 Shallot, Large & Sliced Thin
10 Cremini Mushrooms, Sliced
½ Cup Red Wine, Dry
1 Cup Arborio Rice
1 ½ 2 Cups Vegetable Broth
½ Cup Parmesan Cheese, Grated
1 Tablespoon Parsley, Freshly Chopped
1 Teaspoon Sea Salt, Fine
Black Pepper to Taste

Directions:
Heat your oil in a skillet using high heat, and then add in your shallot. Cook for three to five minutes or until softened.
Add your mushrooms and red wine, simmering until the wine evaporates.
Add in your rice, cooking for three more minutes.

Add in a half a cup of your broth, cooking and stirring until it's been absorbed. Repeat until your risotto is tender, but it shouldn't be mushy. This should take roughly twenty minutes.
Remove from heat, sprinkling with parsley, parmesan, salt and pepper. Serve warm.

NUTRITION: Calories: 320Kcal Proteins: 10g Carbohydrates: 829g Fat: 11g

Slow Cooker Shawarma

Prep time: 10 minutes **Cook time:** 8 hours **Serves** 6

Ingredients:
1 tablespoon fine Himalayan salt
1 tablespoon ground black pepper
1 tablespoon ground cumin
1 teaspoon ground cardamom
½ teaspoon ground nutmeg
3 pounds (1.4 kg) boneless chuck short rib or shoulder ¼ cup coconut vinegar or red wine vinegar
3 tablespoons avocado oil
5 cloves garlic, peeled
1 large onion, quartered
1 lemon, quartered
1 navel orange, quartered

Directions:
1. In a small bowl, mix together the salt, pepper, cumin, cardamom, and nutmeg. Rub the spice mixture all over the meat. 2. Place the meat in a large bowl and drizzle the vinegar and oil all over it. Add the garlic, onion, and citrus. Toss to combine, squeezing some juice out of the fruit. Cover and set in the refrigerator to marinate overnight. 3. When you're ready to cook, put everything in the slow cooker, meat on the bottom, citrus and onion quarters on top. Cook on low for 8 hours. 4. Discard the large pieces of citrus. Use two forks to shred the beef. If you like crispy beef, you can spread it on a sheet pan and broil it for 5 minutes to get delicious crispy tips. Divide the shredded beef among five or six plates, spoon the delicious slow cooker sauce over the meat, and serve. 5. Store leftovers in an airtight container in the fridge for up to 5 days or in the freezer for up to 30 days. To thaw and reheat, place in a preheated 400ºF (205ºC) oven for 10 to 20 minutes.

NUTRITION: Calories: 496 fat: 28g protein: 54g carbs: 8g fiber: 2g sugar: 2g sodium: 600mg

Garlicky Lamb Stew

Prep time: 15 minutes **Cook time:** 15 minutes **Serves** 4

Ingredients:
1 pound (454 g) ground lamb
1 tablespoon extravirgin olive oil
1 onion, chopped
1 teaspoon dried oregano
½ teaspoon sea salt
¼ teaspoon freshly ground black pepper
1 (28 ounces / 794 g) can chopped tomatoes, drained 5 garlic cloves, minced

Directions:

1. In a large nonstick skillet over mediumhigh heat, cook the lamb for about 5 minutes, crumbling it with a wooden spoon until it browns. Drain the fat and remove the lamb to a dish. 2. Return the skillet to the heat, add the olive oil, and heat it until it shimmers. 3. Add the onion, oregano, salt, and pepper. Cook for 5 minutes, stirring, until the onions are soft. 4. Return the lamb to the skillet and stir in the tomatoes. Cook for 3 minutes, stirring occasionally, or until heated through. 5. Add the garlic. Cook for 30 seconds, stirring constantly.

NUTRITION: Calories: 295 fat: 12g protein: 34g carbs: 12g fiber: 3g sugar: 7g sodium: 332mg

Pork Sausage

Prep time: 10 minutes **Cook time:** 15 minutes **Makes** 10 patties

Ingredients:
2 pounds (907 g) ground pork
2 ribs celery, minced
4 cloves garlic, minced
2 teaspoons Dijon mustard
2 teaspoons fine Himalayan salt
1 teaspoon dried thyme leaves
1 teaspoon ground black pepper
¼ teaspoon ginger powder
¼ teaspoon ground cinnamon
Pinch of ground nutmeg

Directions:
1. Place all of the ingredients in a large bowl and mix thoroughly with your hands. 2. Heat a large castiron skillet over medium heat. While it heats, shape the pork mixture into patties, about ¼ cup per patty. 3. When the skillet is hot, place four or five patties in the pan, without crowding the pan. Cook the patties for 6 minutes per side, or until the internal temperature reaches 165ºF (74ºC). Repeat with the remaining patties. 4. This sausage stores well side by side in an airtight container in the refrigerator for up to 5 days or in the freezer for up to 30 days. To reheat, place in a preheated 350ºF (180ºC) oven for 8 to 10 minutes.

NUTRITION: Calories: 157 fat: 12g protein: 9g carbs: 2g fiber: 0g sugar: 0g sodium: 364mg

Yogurt with Dates

Prep time: 5 minutes. **Cook time:** 0 minutes. **Serves:** 4

Ingredients:
2 cups coconut yogurt, unsweetened
¼ cup chopped almonds
¼ cup chopped walnuts
2 pitted dates, chopped
½ teaspoon ground cinnamon

Directions:
In a suitable bowl, stir together the yogurt, almonds, walnuts, dates, and cinnamon. Serve immediately.

NUTRITION: Calories 161; Fat 10.7g; Sodium 25mg; Carbs 11.8g; Fiber 2g; Sugars 8.9g; Protein 6.3g

Chai Pudding

Prep time: 5 minutes **Cook time:** 0 minutes **Servings:** 2

Ingredients:
½ cup 2 tablespoons canned coconut milk
½ teaspoon sweet spice blend
1 teaspoon pure maple syrup
2 tablespoons chia seeds

Directions:
In a small pot, over low heat, warm milk just until it achieves a liquid and uniform consistency.
In a suitable bowl or mason jar, combine milk, sweet spice blend, maple syrup, and chia seeds. Stir well to combine. Place in refrigerator with a tightfitting lid for at least 2 hours.
Remove from refrigerator and eat as is.

NUTRITION: Calories 284; Fat 23g; Sodium 14mg; Carbs 17.5g; Fiber 11.1g; Sugars 4g; Protein 6.1g

Lemon and Mint Breezy Blueberry

Prep Time: 10 minutes **Cook time:** 0 minutes **Serves** 1

Ingredients:
Handful of mint
1 teaspoon chia seeds
1 tablespoon lemon juice
1 cup of coconut water
1 cup strawberries
1 cup blueberries

Directions:
Add in the listed ingredients to a blender
Blend until you have a smooth and creamy texture Serve chilled and enjoy!

NUTRITION: Calories: 169 Fat: 13g Protein: 6g Total Carbs: 11g Fiber: 10g Net Carbs: 1g

Spinach Soup with Gnocchi

Servings: 4 **Cooking Time:** 25 Minutes

Ingredients:
1 tsp olive oil
1 cup red bell peppers
Sea salt and pepper to taste
2 garlic cloves, minced
2 carrots, chopped
3 cups vegetable broth
1 cup gnocchi
¾ cup nondairy milk
¼ cup nutritional yeast

2 cups chopped spinach
¼ cup black olives, chopped
Croutons, for topping

Directions:
Heat the oil in a pot over medium heat. Place in bell peppers, garlic, carrots, and salt and cook for 5 minutes. Stir in broth. Bring to a boil.
Put in gnocchi, cook for 10 minutes. Add in spinach and cook for 5 minutes. Stir in milk, nutritional yeast, and olives. Top with croutons.

NUTRITION: Calories: 205;Fat: 7g;Protein: 7g;Carbs: 28g.

Meatballs

Prep Time: 10 minutes **Cooking Time**: 25 minutes **Serve**: 4

Ingredients:
2 lbs ground beef
½ tsp ground ginger
1 tbsp garlic, minced
¼ cup fresh cilantro, chopped
1 lime zest
Pepper
Salt

Directions:
Preheat the oven to 350 F.
Line baking sheet with parchment paper and set aside.
In a mixing bowl, mix meat, ginger, garlic, cilantro, lime zest, pepper, and salt until well combined.
Make small balls from the meat mixture, place them onto the prepared baking sheet, and bake for 2325 minutes.
Serve and enjoy.
NUTRITION: Calories 426 Fat 12 g Carbohydrates 2 g Sugar 0.1 g Protein 69 g Cholesterol 203 mg

Ginger Honey Pork Chops

Prep Time: 10 minutes **Cooking Time**: 15 minutes Serve: 6

Ingredients:
6 pork chops
2 tbsp Dijon mustard
½ cup honey
2 tbsp ginger, grated
Pepper
Salt

Directions:
Preheat the grill.
Mix honey, Dijon mustard, ginger, pepper, and salt in a small bowl.
Brush pork chops with honey mixture and place onto the hot grill, and cook for 56 minutes on each side.

Serve and enjoy.

NUTRITION: Calories 352 Fat 20.2 g Carbohydrates 28 g Sugar 23 g Protein 15 g Cholesterol 69 m

Quick & Juicy Lamb Chops

Prep Time: 10 minutes **Cooking Time**: 8 minutes **Serve**: 4

Ingredients:
1 ½ lbs lamb chops
1 tbsp coconut oil
½ tsp turmeric
3 garlic cloves, minced
1 tbsp Canola oil
¼ tsp paprika
1 tbsp fresh lime juice
1 ½ tsp sea salt

Directions:
Mixing lamb chops paprika, turmeric, garlic, olive oi, lemon juice, and salt in a mixing bowl. Cover and place in refrigerator for 1 hour.
Melt coconut oil in a pan over medium heat.
Place marinated lamb chops in a pan and cook for 34 minutes on each side.
Serve and enjoy.

NUTRITION: Calories 386Fat 15 gCarbohydrates 4 g Sugar 0.5 g Protein 41 g Cholesterol 153 mg

Salmon and Feta Cheese and Papillote

Ingredients:
1 tablespoon English mustard
2 tablespoons white vinegar
½ tsp. honey
Coarse salt and freshly ground pepper
5 tablespoons extravirgin olive oil
4 pcs. of 4 oz. salmon fillets
20 to 24 thin asparagus spears, trimmed 12 cherry tomatoes, halved
20 green olives, pitted
4 artichoke hearts, steamed and quartered 8 basil leaves, torn
¾ cup feta cheese

Directions:
Preheat your oven to 350 degrees Fahrenheit Combine the mustard, vinegar, honey, pepper and salt
Slowly add in the olive oil to this mixture by whisking it.
Season the salmon with salt and pepper
Cut for pieces of parchment paper 16 by 18 inches.
Fold each sheet in half lengthwise.
Evenly divide the asparagus among the four pieces of parchment paper.
Place a salmon on top of each of them.
Drizzle 1 tablespoon of vinaigrette.

Cook the salmon with tomatoes, olives, artichokes, basil and feta cheese.
Add another tablespoon of vinaigrette
Fold the parchment paper in half and seal the edges off by crimping them.
Transfer to a baking sheet and roast for 27 minutes.
Pace the packets on a plate and cut an x mark on top to release the steam.

Salad

Chopped Thai Salad

Prep Time: 25 minutes **Cook time**: 0 minutes **Serves** 6

Dressing:
½ cup extravirgin olive oil
3 tablespoons filtered water
2 tablespoons coconut aminos
1 tablespoon apple cider vinegar
1 tablespoon freshly squeezed lime juice
1 tablespoon raw honey
1 teaspoon sesame oil
1 teaspoon garlic powder
Dash ground ginger

Salad:
2 cups shredded kale, stemmed and thoroughly washed 2 cups shredded napa cabbage
2 cups shredded red cabbage
4 scallions, sliced
1 cup shredded carrots
1 red bell pepper, julienned
1 yellow bell pepper, julienned
1 cucumber, julienned
½ cup fresh cilantro leaves, roughly chopped
½ cup cashews, roughly chopped

Make the Dressing: In a medium bowl, whisk the olive oil, water, coconut aminos, vinegar, lime juice, honey, sesame oil, garlic powder, and ginger
until combined. Set aside.

Make the Salad:
1. In a large bowl, mix the kale, napa cabbage, red cabbage, scallions, carrots, red bell pepper, yellow bell pepper, and cucumber. Top with the cilantro and cashews. Pour the dressing over the salad, toss well, and serve immediately.

NUTRITION:
Calories: 272 fat: 22g protein: 3g carbs: 16g fiber: 4g sugar: 7g sodium: 40mg

Healthy Tuna Salad

Prep Time: 10 minutes **Cooking Time**: 5 minutes **Serve**: 2

Ingredients:
6 oz can tuna, drained & flaked
1 fresh lime juice
2 tbsp unsweetened dried cranberries
1 tbsp Dijon mustard
2 tbsp onion, minced
3 tbsp mayonnaise
Pepper
Salt

Directions:
Add tuna and remaining ingredients into the bowl and mix until well combined.
Cover and place in the fridge for 1 hour.
Serve and enjoy.

NUTRITION: Calories 117 Fat 5 g Carbohydrates 2 g Sugar 8 g Protein 13 g Cholesterol 17 mg

Massaged Swiss Chard Salad with Chopped Egg

Prep Time: 25 minutes **Cook time**: 0 minutes Serves 4

Dressing:
¼ cup olive oil
3 tablespoons freshly squeezed lemon juice
2 teaspoons raw honey
1 teaspoon Dijon mustard
Sea salt, to taste

Salad:
5 cups chopped Swiss chard
3 large hardboiled eggs, peeled and chopped
1 English cucumber, diced
½ cup sliced radishes
½ cup chopped pecans

For the Dressing:

In a bowl, whisk the olive oil, lemon juice, honey, and mustard. Season with salt and set it aside.

For the Salad:

In a bowl, toss the Swiss chard and dressing together for about 4 minutes, or until the greens start to soften. Divide the greens evenly among four plates. Top each salad with egg, cucumber, radishes, and pecans.

NUTRITION: Calories: 241 fat: 21g protein: 7g carbs: 9g fiber: 2g sugar: 5g sodium: 163mg

Veggie Salad

Prep time: 10 minutes. **Cooking time:** 0 minutes. **Servings:** 4

Ingredients:
2 Carrots, peeled and grated
1 avocado, pitted, peeled, and chopped
½ green cabbage head, shredded
2 Strawberries, halved
Salt and black pepper to taste
¼ teaspoon matcha powder
1 teaspoon maple syrup
¼ Tablespoon white wine vinegar
1 tablespoon Dijon mustard
¼ cup lemon juice
¾ cup olive oil

Directions:
1. In a bowl, whisk together the lemon juice with oil, vinegar, matcha tea powder, maple syrup, mustard, salt, and pepper. In a salad bowl, mix avocado with cabbage, strawberries, and carrots.
2. Add lemon juice, oil, vinegar, matcha powder, maple syrup, mustard, salt, and pepper. Toss well and serve for lunch.
3. Enjoy!

NUTRITION: Calories: 211 Fat: 4 g Fiber: 2 g Carbs: 8 g Protein: 7g

Grilled Eggplant Salad

Prep time: 10 minutes. **Cooking time:** 20 minutes. **Servings:** 4

Ingredients:
1 tomato, diced
1 eggplant, pricked
A pinch of salt and black pepper
¼ teaspoon ground turmeric
1(½) teaspoon red wine vinegar
½ teaspoon chopped oregano
½ tablespoon olive oil
2 garlic cloves, minced
½ tablespoon chopped parsley
½ Tablespoon chopped capers

Directions:
1. Preheat your grill over medium-high heat, then add the eggplant and cook for 15 minutes, flipping occasionally. Scoop the flesh, roughly slice it, and place it in a bowl. Toss tomatoes, turmeric, garlic, vinegar, oregano, parsley, oil, capers with salt, and pepper to taste. Enjoy!

NUTRITION: Calories: 192 Fat: 7 g Fiber: 6 g Carbs: 12 g Protein: 7 g

Blackberry Salad

Prep time: 5 minutes. **Cooking time:** 0 minutes. **Servings**: 1

Ingredients:
¼ cup sliced almonds
¼ cup blackberries
¼ cup strawberries, halved
1 banana, peeled and sliced
Ground cinnamon, a pinch

Directions:
1. In a bowl, mix the blackberries with strawberries, cinnamon, banana, and almonds. Serve for breakfast.
2. Enjoy!

NUTRITION: Calories: 90 Fat: 0.3 g Fiber: 1 g Carbs: 0 g Protein: 5 g

Zucchini Salad

Prep time: 10 minutes. **Cooking time:** 0 minutes. **Servings**: 4

Ingredients:
2 Zucchinis, spiralized
1 cup beets, baked, peeled, and grated
½ bunch kale, chopped
½ tablespoon olive oil
For the tahini sauce:
1 tablespoon maple syrup
Juice of 1 lime
¼ inch fresh ginger, grated
1/3 cup sesame seed paste

Directions:
Combine the zucchinis, beets, kale, and oil in a salad dish. Whisk together the maple syrup, lime juice, ginger, and sesame paste in a separate small bowl. Toss the salad with the dressing and serve for breakfast.

NUTRITION: Calories: 183 Fat: 3 g Fiber: 2 g Carbs: 7 g Protein: 9 g

Nutritious Salad with Lentil And Beets

Servings: 4 **Cooking Time:** 0 Minute

Ingredients:
4 cups baby spinach
15 ounces can lentils, drained and rinsed 4 cooked peeled beets, 1 cut into 8 pieces 1 small red onion, sliced
cup extra-virgin olive oil
1 tablespoon apple cider vinegar
1 teaspoon salt
¼ teaspoon black pepper, freshly ground

Directions:
1. Arrange the spinach leaves on a serving platter or in a bowl.
2. Top with the lentils, beets, and red onion.
3. Whisk together the olive oil, cider vinegar, salt, and pepper in a small bowl.
4. Drizzle the salad with the dressing and serve.

NUTRITION:
Per Serving: Calories: 320 ;Fat: 18g ;Protein: 11g ;Carbs: 29g .

Carrot and Raisin Salad

Prep Time: 12 minutes   **Cook time**: 0 minutes   **Serves** 6

4 cups shredded carrots
1 cup raisins, chopped
¾ cup sunflower seeds
¼ cup maple syrup, plus additional as needed
¼ cup freshly squeezed lemon juice, plus additional as needed In a large bowl, mix together the carrots, raisins, and sunflower seeds.
Stir in the maple syrup and lemon juice. Taste, and add more lemon juice or maple syrup if necessary.

NUTRITION: Calories: 173   fat: 3g   protein: 3g   carbs: 37g   fiber: 3g   sugar: 26g   sodium: 57mg

Pineapple Apple Salad

Prep Time: 10 minutes **Cooking Time**: 5 minutes **Serve:** 4

Ingredients:
1 cup crushed pineapple, drained
2 cups coconut yogurt
¾ cup walnuts, chopped
½ cup raisins
¼ cup celery, diced
4 medium apples, chopped

Directions:
Add crushed pineapple and remaining ingredients into the mixing bowl and mix well.
Serve and enjoy.

NUTRITION: Calories 343 Fat 14 g Carbohydrates 53 g Sugar 39 g Protein 6 g Cholesterol 0 mg

Perfect Chicken Salad

Prep Time: 10 minutes **Cooking Time**: 5 minutes **Serve:** 4

Ingredients:
For salad:
2 cups cooked chicken, shredded
¼ cup raisins
1 green onion, chopped

1 cup shredded cabbage
1 cup shredded carrots
For dressing:
1/3 cup olive oil
2 tbsp apple cider vinegar
1 tsp honey
1 garlic clove, minced
1 tbsp tahini
1 tsp turmeric
¼ tsp kosher salt

Directions:
Add all salad ingredients into the large bowl and mix well.
In a small bowl, whisk together dressing ingredients, pour over salad, and toss well.
Serve and enjoy.

NUTRITION: Calories 326Fat 21 g Carbohydrates 11 g Sugar 9 g Protein 28 g Cholesterol 54 mg

Fish and Seafood

Tuna and Kale

Prep Time: 5 minutes **Cooking Time**: 20 minutes **Servings**: 4

Ingredients
1 pound tuna fillets, boneless, skinless and cubed A pinch of salt and black pepper
2 tablespoons olive oil
1 cup kale, torn
½ cup cherry tomatoes, cubed
1 yellow onion, chopped

Directions
Heat up a pan with the oil over medium heat, add the onion and sauté for 5 minutes.
Add the tuna and the other ingredients, toss, cook everything for 15
minutes more, divide between plates and serve.

NUTRITION: Calories: 251Fat: 4Fiber: 7Carbs: 14Protein: 7

Veggie, Salmon & Quinoa Bowl

Servings: 4 **Cooking Time**: 15 Minutes

Ingredients:
½ cup toasted slivered almonds
1 lb cooked salmon, flaked
4 cups cooked quinoa
6 radishes, thinly sliced
1 zucchini, cut into halfmoons

3 cups arugula
1 red onion, sliced thin
½ cup almond oil
1 tsp sugarfree hot sauce
1 tbsp apple cider vinegar
1 tsp sea salt

Directions:
Stir the flaked salmon, cooked quinoa, radishes, zucchini, arugula, and red onion in a large bowl. Pour in the almond oil, hot sauce, apple cider vinegar, and sea salt and toss to combine. Divide the mixture between four bowls. Top with slivered almonds and serve immediately.

NUTRITION: Per Serving: Calories: 770;Fat: 50g;Protein: 38g;Carbs: 45g.

Baked Cod Fillets with Mushroom

Servings: 4 **Cooking Time**: 30 Minutes

Ingredients:
8 oz shiitake mushrooms, sliced
1 ½ lb cod fillets
1 leek, sliced thin
Sea salt and pepper to taste
1 lemon, zested
2 tbsp extravirgin olive oil
1 tbsp coconut aminos
1 tsp sweet paprika
½ cup vegetable broth

Directions:
Preheat your oven to 375ºF. In a baking dish, combine the olive oil, leek, mushrooms, coconut aminos, lemon zest, paprika, and salt. Place the cod fillets over and sprinkle it with salt and pepper. Pour in the vegetable broth. Bake for 1520 minutes, or until the cod is firm but cooked through. Serve and enjoy!

NUTRITION: Calories: 220;Fat: 5g;Protein: 32g;Carbs: 12g.

Broiled Sea Bass

Servings: 2

Ingredients:
2 minced garlic cloves
Pepper
1 tablespoon lemon juice
2 white sea bass fillets
¼ teaspoon herb seasoning blend

Directions:
Spray a broiler pan with some olive oil and place the fillets on it.
Sprinkle the lemon juice, garlic and the spices over the fillets.

Broil for about 10 min or until the fish is golden.
Serve over a bed of sautéed spinach if desired.

NUTRITION: Calories: 169, Fat:3 g, Carbs:0.34 g, Protein:13 g, Sugars:0.2 g, Sodium:323 mg

Greek Baked Cod

Prep Time: 10 minutes **Cooking time**: 15 minutes **Servings**: 4

Add a little of the Mediterranean touch to your meal.

Ingredients:
1 ½ lb. cod fillet pieces (4–6 pieces)
5 garlic cloves, peeled and minced
¼ C. fresh parsley leaves, chopped
Lemon Juice Mixture:
5 tbsp. fresh lemon juice
5 tbsp. extra virgin olive oil
2 tbsp. vegan butter, melted
For coating:
⅓ C. allpurpose flour
1 tsp. coriander, ground
¾ tsp. sweet Spanish paprika
¾ tsp. cumin, ground
¾ tsp. salt
½ tsp. black pepper

Directions:
Preheat oven to 400°F.
Mix lemon juice, olive oil, and melted butter, set aside.
In another shallow bowl, mix allpurpose flour, spices, salt, and pepper, set next to the lemon bowl to create a station.
Pat the fish fillet dry, then dip the fish in the lemon juice mixture then dip it in the flour mixture, and brush off extra flour.
In a castiron skillet over mediumhigh heat, add 2 tbsp. olive oil.
Once heated, add in the fish and sear on each side for color but do not thoroughly cook, then remove from heat.
With the remaining lemon juice mixture, add the minced garlic and mix.
Drizzle all over the fish fillets.
Bake for 10 minutes, until it begins to flake easily with a fork.
Allow the dish to cool completely.
Distribute among the containers, store for 2–3 days.
To serve: reheat in the microwave for 1–2 minutes or until heated through. Sprinkle chopped parsley over. Enjoy!

NUTRITION: Calories: 3804 kcal Fat: 26 g Protein: 323 g Carbs: 16 g Sodium: 629 mg

Mussels and Clams in White Wine

Prep Time: 10 minutes **Cooking time**: 10 minutes **Servings**: 4

Shellfish are loaded with healthy proteins that help you manage excess weight and improve your immune function.

Ingredients:
2 tbsp. extravirgin olive oil
1 shallot, minced
2 garlic cloves, minced
1 C. dry white wine
½ tsp. red pepper flakes
1lb. clams, scrubbed
1lb. mussels, scrubbed and debearded
¼ C. arugula, chopped

Directions:
In a large, deep skillet, heat the olive oil over low heat. Cook the shallot for about 5 minutes, until it starts to soften. Add the garlic and cook for 1 minute.
Stir in the white wine and red pepper flakes and cook for 1 minute to allow the alcohol to evaporate. Increase the heat to medium and add the clams and mussels.
Cover and steam for 3–5 minutes until the shellfish have opened.
Discard any that do not open. If you need more liquid to steam them, add some water.
Remove the shellfish from the pan and top with the sauce from the pan and chopped arugula.
Variation tip: You can enjoy this dish as is, or serve it over linguine if you like.

NUTRITION: Calories: 1897 kcal Total Fat: 79 g Saturated Fat: 28 g Protein: 39 g Total Carbohydrates: 77 g Fiber: 0.32 g Sugar: 0.56 g Cholesterol: 24 mg

Spicy Cod

Servings: 4

Ingredients:
2 tablespoons Fresh chopped parsley
2 lbs. cod fillets
2 c. low sodium salsa
1 tablespoon flavorless oil

Directions:
Preheat the oven to 350°F.
In a large, deep baking dish drizzle the oil along the bottom. Place the cod fillets in the dish. Pour the salsa over the fish. Cover with foil for 20 minutes. Remove the foil last 10 minutes of cooking.
Bake in the oven for 20 – 30 minutes, until the fish is flaky.
Serve with white or brown rice. Garnish with parsley.

NUTRITION: Calories: 110, Fat:11 g, Carbs:83 g, Protein:15 g, Sugars:0 g, Sodium:122 mg

Creamy Turmeric Shrimp

Prep Time: 10 minutes **Cooking Time**: 8 minutes Serve: 4

Ingredients:
1 lb shrimp
1 tbsp cornstarch
1/8 tsp cayenne
1 tsp olive oil
2 tsp turmeric
14 oz can coconut milk
Salt

Directions:
Heat oil in a pan over medium heat.
Add shrimp to the pan and cook until shrimp turns pink in color.
Remove from pan and set aside.
Add milk, cayenne, turmeric, and salt to the same pan and stir well.
Stir cornstarch with ¼ cup water, add it to the pan and continue until sauce thickens.
Add shrimp and stir well.
Serve and enjoy.

NUTRITION: Calories 352 Fat 24 g Carbohydrates 1 g Sugar 0.1 g Protein 29 g Cholesterol 239 mg

Salmon Balls

Prep Time: 6minutes **Total time:** 19minutes **Yield:** 2servings

Ingredients:
Salt and ground black pepper to
2 tbsp. water
taste
2 tbsp. lemon juice
½ tsp dried cilantro
½ tsp paprika
½ tsp ginger powder
3 tbsp. coconut oil
½ c. heavy cream
1 garlic clove
1 egg
1 avocado
2 tbsp. keto mayo
1 salmon

Directions:
Drain the salmon, chop it. Mince the garlic clove, peel the avocado. In a bowl, Mix the garlic, egg, mayo, and fish, season with salt, paprika, and ginger, mix well. Make 4 balls of it. Using a skillet, preheat the oil at medium heat. Fry the balls for 46minutes on each side.
Meanwhile, put the lemon juice, cilantro, avocado, heavy cream, and 1 tbsp.
Of oil in a blender. Pulse well.

Serve the balls with the sauce.

NUTRITION: Carbs: 3,9 g Fats: 50 g Protein: 20,1 g Calories: 555

Cod and Mushrooms Mix

Prep Time: 10 minutes **Cooking time**: 25 minutes **Servings**: 4

This delectable recipe adds some earthiness to your meal and nutrients to your body.

Ingredients:
2 cod fillets, boneless
4 tbsp. olive oil
4 oz. mushrooms, sliced
Sea salt and black pepper to taste
12 cherry tomatoes, halved
8 oz. lettuce leaves, torn
1 avocado, pitted, peeled, and cubed
1 red chili pepper, chopped
1 tbsp. cilantro, chopped
2 tbsp. balsamic vinegar
1oz. feta cheese, crumbled

Directions:
Put the fish in a roasting pan, brush it with 2 tbsp. oil, sprinkle salt and pepper all over and broil under mediumhigh heat for 15
minutes.
Meantime, heat up a pan with the rest of the oil over medium heat; add the mushrooms, stir, and sauté for 5 minutes.
Now add the rest of the ingredients, toss, cook for 5 minutes more, and divide between plates.
Top with the fish and serve right away.

NUTRITION: Calories: 2869 kcal Fat: 20.7 g Fiber: 67 g carbs: 45 g Protein: 137 g

Creamy Sea Bass Mix

Servings: 4

Ingredients:
1 tablespoon chopped parsley
2 tablespoons avocado oil
1 c. coconut cream
1 tablespoon lime juice
1 chopped yellow onion
¼ teaspoon black pepper
4 boneless sea bass fillets

Directions:
Heat up a pan with the oil over medium heat, add the onion, toss and sauté for 2
minutes.
Add the fish and cook it for 4 minutes on each side.

Add the rest of the ingredients, cook everything for 4 minutes more, divide between plates and serve.

NUTRITION: Calories: 283, Fat:13 g, Carbs:15 g, Protein:8 g, Sugars:6 g, Sodium:508 mg

Dessert and Smothie

Tropical Popsicles

Prep Time: 10 Minutes **Cooking Time**: 10Minutes Servings: 6

Ingredients:
2 Kiwi, sliced
3 cups Pineapple, chopped
2 tbsp. Coconut Oil
2 tsp. Turmeric
½ tsp. Black Pepper

Directions:
First, place all the ingredients to make the popsicles excluding the kiwi in a highspeed blender for 2 minutes or until you get a smooth mixture.
Next, pour the smoothie into the popsicle molds.
After that, insert the kiwi slices into the molds and then place the frames in the freezer until set.

NUTRITION: Calories: 101 Kcal Protein: 0.5g Carbohydrates: 15g Fat:4g

Mango & Kale Smoothie

Prep time: 15 minutes **Cooking Time**: 20 minutes **Servings**: 1

Ingredients:
1 cup baby kale
1 cup frozen mango chunks
1 small banana, sliced
1 cup fresh orange juice

Directions:
Combine the kale, mango, banana, and orange juice in a blender. Blend on medium-low speed, scraping down the sides as needed until well blended.
Increase the speed to medium-high and blend until the mixture is extremely smooth.

Fancy Cold Soup Smoothie

Servings: 1 **Cooking Time**: 15 Minutes

Ingredients:
Frozen Veggie Mix:
2 cups butternut squash, diced
1 cup broccoli florets
1 cup onions, diced
4 cloves garlic, peeled
3 cups water
Smoothie:
1 bag steamed and then frozen mixed veggies 1½ cups bone broth or water

2 tablespoons collagen peptides
1 tablespoon MCT oil or MCT oil powder
2 teaspoons apple cider vinegar
½ teaspoon thyme or oregano, dried
½ teaspoon Himalayan salt, fine
½ teaspoon turmeric powder

Directions:
1. Make the frozen veggie mix. Place all of the veggies in a large skillet with a tight-fitting lid. Add the water and bring to a boil. Cover and steam for 15 minutes or until the butternut squash is fork-tender. Remove from the heat, drain, and let cool.
2. Divide the cooled vegetables into five resealable plastic bags, about 1
cup per bag. Seal and pop in the freezer for 1 hour before making your smoothie.
3. Place 1 bag of frozen veggies in a blender when you're ready to make a smoothie and add the smoothie ingredients then blend until smooth.
Drink. Store any leftovers in the fridge in an airtight container for up to 4 days.
NUTRITION: Per Serving: Calories: 304 ;Fat: 18g ;Protein: 20g;Carbs: 9g.

Almond Butter Chocolate Cups

Prep Time: 10 minutes   **Cook time**: 5 minutes   **Makes** 9 cups 6 ounces (170 g) dark chocolate, chopped

Ingredients:
½ cup natural almond butter
2 tablespoons raw honey
½ teaspoon vanilla extract
Dash salt

Directions:
Line 9 cups of a mini muffin tin with mini paper liners.
In a small saucepan over low heat, slowly melt the chocolate. Use half of the chocolate among the mini muffin cups. Set the rest of the chocolate aside.
In a small bowl, stir together the almond butter, honey, and vanilla.
Divide the mixture into 9 portions and roll each into a small ball. Drop 1
ball into each muffin cup.
Drizzle the remaining chocolate into each cup, covering the almond butter balls.
Sprinkle each lightly with the salt.
Refrigerate until solid.

NUTRITION: calories: 193 fat: 16g protein: 5g carbs: 14g fiber: 0g sugar: 9g sodium: 22mg

Vanilla Cookies with Chocolate Chips

Prep Time: 15 minutes   **Cook time:** 10 minutes   **Makes** 12 cookies ¾ cup creamy almond butter

Ingredients:
½ cup coconut sugar
¼ cup cocoa powder
2 teaspoons vanilla extract

1 egg
1 egg yolk
1 teaspoon baking soda
¼ teaspoon salt
½ cup semisweet chocolate chips
Dash sea salt (optional)

Directions:
Preheat the oven to 350ºF (180ºC).
Line 2 baking sheets with parchment paper.
In a medium bowl, cream together the almond butter, coconut sugar, cocoa powder, and vanilla.
In a small bowl, whisk the egg and egg yolk. Add the eggs to the almond butter mixture and stir to combine.
Stir in the baking soda, salt, and chocolate chips until well mixed. Divide the dough into 12 pieces. Roll the dough into balls and put 6 on each prepared pan.
Bake for 9 to 10 minutes. Let the cookies rest on the pans for 5 minutes, where they'll continue to cook. Sprinkle each with a dash of sea salt (if using). Remove to a cooling rack.

NUTRUTION: Calories: 307   fat: 20g   protein: 9g   carbs: 28g   fiber: 4g   sugar: 20g sodium: 364mg

Mango, Cucumber and Spinach Smoothie

Prep time: 10-minutes   **Total time:** 10-minutes   **Yield:** 1 serving

Ingredients:
1 c. water
1 c. orange juice, fresh
3 c. baby spinach
1 c. frozen mango, cubed and deseeded
2 apples, cored and chopped
1 cucumber, ends removed and chopped roughly roughly

Directions:
Add all ingredients to a blender. Blend until smooth and creamy. Serve and enjoy.
NUTRITION: Calories 455 Fat 2g Carbs 111g Protein 8g Sugar: 21g Fiber 15g Sodium 90mg

Apple Muesli

Servings: 4 To 6 **Cooking Time**: 0 Minutes

Ingredients:
- 2 cups gluten-free rolled oats
- ¼ cup no-added-sugar apple juice
- 1¾ cups coconut milk
- 1 tablespoon apple cider vinegar
- 1 apple, cored and chopped
- Dash ground cinnamon

Directions:
1. Combine the oats, apple juice, coconut milk, and apple cider vinegar in a bowl. Stir to mix well. Wrap the bowl in plastic and refrigerate overnight.
2. Remove the bowl from the refrigerator. Top with apple and sprinkle with cinnamon, then serve.

NUTRITION: calories: 212 ; fat: 3.7g ; protein: 6.1g ; carbs: 38.9g ; fiber: 6.0g ; sugar: 10.0g ; sodium: 73mg

Carrot Cake

Servings: 6 Cooking Time: 0 Minutes

Ingredients:
- 1 cup pineapple, dried and chopped
- 2 carrots, chopped
- 1 ½ cups coconut flour
- 1 cup dates, pitted
- ½ cup shredded coconut, unsweetened
- ½ teaspoon ground cinnamon

Directions:
1. Put carrots in your food processor, pulse then add the flour, dates, pineapple, coconut and cinnamon. Pulse again and spoon this into a cake pan, spread evenly and keep in the freezer for 3 hours before serving.
2. Enjoy!

NUTRITION: calories 160, fat 7, fiber 4, carbs 11, protein 4.

Lemony Steamed Asparagus

Servings: 4 **Cooking Time:** 0 Minutes

Ingredients:
1 pound asparagus, woody ends removed Juice from
½ large lemon
¼ teaspoon kosher salt

Directions:
Add ½ cup water to the inner pot and add the steam rack. Add the asparagus to the steamer basket and place the basket on top of the rack, then steam within 1 minute.
Transfer, and top with lemon juice and salt.

NUTRITION: Calories 13 Fat: 0g Protein: 1g Sodium: 146mg Fiber: 1g Carbohydrates: 3g Sugar: 1g

Spiced Tea Pudding

Prep Time: 10minutes **Total time:** 20minutes **Yield:** 3servings

Ingredients:
1 can coconut milk
½ c. coconut flakes
1 c. almond milk
1 tsp. nutmeg

1 tbsp. Ground cinnamon
½ tsp. cloves
1 tsp. allspice
1 tbsp. Raw honey
tsps. ground ginger
1 tsp. Cardamom
tbsps. pumpkin seeds
1 ½ c. berries
1 tbsp. chia seeds
1 tsp. green tea powder

Directions:
Puree tea powder with coconut milk, almond milk, cinnamon, coconut flakes, nutmeg, allspice, cloves, honey, cardamom, and ginger in your blender, then divide into bowls. Heat a pan over medium heat, add berries until bubbling, then transfer to your blender and pulse well. Divide the berries into the bowls with the coconut milk mix, top with chia seeds and pumpkin seeds and serve.

NUTRITION: Calories 150, Fat 6, Fiber 5, Carbs 14, Protein 8

Fresh Peach Smoothie
Servings: 2 Cooking Time: 5 Minutes

Ingredients:
1 avocado
2 cups baby spinach
1 cup peach chunks
2 cups almond milk
Juice of 1 lime
2 tbsp maple syrup

Directions:
In a food processor, combine avocado, spinach, milk, lime, and maple syrup. Purée until smooth to serve.

NUTRITION: Per Serving: Calories: 886;Fat: 77g;Protein: 9g;Carbs: 53.9g.

Other wonderful recipes

Mushroom Squash with Vegetable Soup
Prep Time: 10 minutes Cook time: 45 minutes Serves 2

Ingredients:
15 dried shiitake mushrooms, soaked in water
6 cups low salt vegetable stock
½ butternut squash, peeled and cubed
1 tablespoon sesame oil

1 onion, quartered and sliced into rings
1 large garlic clove, chopped
4 stems of pak choy or equivalent
1 sprig of thyme or 1 tablespoon dried thyme
1 teaspoon tabasco sauce (optional)

Directions:
Heat sesame oil in a large pan on a medium high heat before sweating the onions and garlic.
Add the vegetable stock and bring to a boil over a high heat before adding the squash.
Turn down heat and allow to simmer for 25 to 30 minutes.
Soak the mushrooms in the water if not already done, and then press out the liquid and add to the stock into the pot.
Use the mushroom water in the stock for extra taste.
Add the rest of the ingredients except for the greens and allow to simmer for a further 15 minutes or until the squash is tender.
Add in the chopped greens and let them wilt before serving. Serve with the tabasco sauce if you like it spicy.

NUTRITION: Calories: 607   Fat: 44g   Protein: 45g   Total Carbs: 6g   Fiber: 3g   Net Carbs: 3g

Baked Navy Beans

Prep Time: 15 minutes.   **Cook time:** 8 hours   **Serves:** 4 to 6

Ingredients:
2 cups dried navy beans, soaked in water overnight, drained, and rinsed 6 cups vegetable broth
¼ cup dried cranberries
1 medium sweet onion, diced
½ cup sugarfree ketchup
3 tablespoons olive oil
2 tablespoons maple syrup
2 tablespoons molasses
1 tablespoon apple cider vinegar
1 teaspoon Dijon mustard
1 teaspoon sea salt
½ teaspoon garlic powder

Directions:
In your slow cooker, combine the beans, broth, cranberries, onion, ketchup, olive oil, maple syrup, molasses, vinegar, mustard, salt, and garlic powder.
Cover the cooker and set to low. Cook for 7 to 8 hours and serve.
Cooking tip: it's extremely important to soak your beans before using them in a recipe. It reduces the phytic acid, reduces cooking time, ensures an even cooking experience, and allows your tummy the best (and least painful) experience as it digests them. You can even use the bowl of your slow cooker the night before to soak your beans in cool water with a dash of salt. Make sure it's at room temperature and the beans get at least an 8hour bath. Rinse them well before using, and discard the soaking water.

NUTRITION: Calories 380; Fat 5g; Sodium 1092mg; Carbs 58g; Fiber 15g; Sugars 11g; Protein 20.6g

Honey Mustard Chicken

Prep Time: 10 minutes **Cooking Time:** 35 minutes **Serve:** 4

Ingredients:
1 ½ lbs chicken thighs
½ tsp Italian seasoning
5 garlic cloves, minced
1 ½ tbsp honey
¼ tsp dried parsley
1 ½ tbsp canola oil
1 ½ tbsp Dijon mustard
Pepper
Salt

Directions:
Preheat the oven to 425 F.
Season chicken with pepper and salt and place it into the baking dish.
Mix remaining ingredients, pour over chicken and bake in a preheated oven for 35 minutes.
Serve and enjoy.

NUTRITION: Calories 403 Fat 11 g Carbohydrates 3 g Sugar 7 g Protein 48 g Cholesterol 151 mg

Cheddar & Kale Frittata

Servings: 6

Ingredients:
1/3 c. sliced scallions
¼ teaspoon pepper
1 diced red pepper
¾ c. nonfat milk
1 c. shredded sharp lowfat cheddar cheese
1 teaspoon olive oil
5 oz. baby kale and spinach
12 eggs

Directions:
preheat the oven to 375 0F.
With olive oil, grease a glass casserole dish.
In a bowl, whisk well all ingredients except for cheese.
Pour egg mixture into the o prepared dish and bake for 35 minutes.
Remove from oven and sprinkle cheese on top and broil for 5 minutes.
Remove from the oven and let it sit for 10 minutes.
Cut up and enjoy.

NUTRITION: Calories: 198, Fat:10 g, Carbs:7 g, Protein:17 g, Sugars:1 g, Sodium:209 mg.

Cabbage Soup

Prep Time: 10 minutes. **Cooking time:** 45 minutes. **Servings:** 4

Ingredients:
2 Cup green cabbage
2 Carrots
1 medium onion
½ Cup mushrooms
2 Cup vegetable stock
1 Cup of water
1 tablespoon thyme
1 tablespoon rosemary
Sea salt to taste
Pepper to taste

Directions:
1 Slice all the vegetables and put them in a pot with the vegetable stock.
2 Add water and put it on medium heat for 15–20 minutes. Let it boil, then lower the heat and add the thyme and rosemary and cook for more than 25 minutes.
3 Season the soup with salt and pepper
4 Serve hot.

NUTRITION: Calories: 90 Carbohydrates: 20 g Protein: 5 g Fat: 1 g Sugar: 0 g Fiber: 5 g Sodium: 521 mg

Chicken with Snow Peas and Brown Rice

Prep Time: 10 minutes   **Cook time:** 5 minutes   **Serves 4**

Ingredients:
1 tablespoon coconut oil
2 cups cooked brown rice
1 cup cooked chicken, cut into ½inch cubes
4 ounces (113 g) snow peas, strings removed
½ cup chicken broth
1 teaspoon salt
½ teaspoon ground ginger
1 teaspoon toasted sesame oil
1 teaspoon coconut aminos
2 scallions, sliced

Directions:
In a large pan over high heat, melt the coconut oil. Add the rice and chicken. Sauté for about 2 minutes. Add the snow peas, chicken broth, salt, and ginger. Cover the pan, reduce the heat to low, and cook for 3 minutes, or until the snow peas turn bright green.
Remove the pan from the heat. Stir in the sesame oil, coconut aminos, and scallions.

NUTRITION: calories: 285 fat: 7g protein: 15g carbs: 39g fiber: 3g sugar: 1g sodium: 705mg

Beef and Mushroom Pasta

Prep Time: 10 minutes **Cooking Time:** 20 minutes **Servings:** 4

Ingredients:
1 tablespoon unsalted butter
1 cup thinly sliced mushrooms
½ onion, finely chopped
8 ounces ground beef
1 teaspoon salt
½ teaspoon dried oregano
¼ teaspoon freshly ground black pepper
2 cups chicken broth or water
8 ounces glutenfree elbow macaroni
¼ cup grated sheep's milk pecorino cheese

Directions :
In a large pot, melt the butter over high heat.
Add the mushrooms and onion and sauté until the softened, about 3 minutes.
Crumble the ground beef into the pot, and add the salt, oregano, and pepper.
Cook the beef until browned on all sides, 3 to 4 minutes total. If desired, drain any extra Fat: that may accumulate in the pot.
Add the broth and macaroni and bring to a boil. Cook, uncovered, until the macaroni is tender, about 8 minutes.
Sprinkle with the cheese and serve.

NUTRITION: Calories: 370Total Fat: 11gTotal Carbohydrates: 44gSugar: 2gFiber: 6g Protein: 23g Sodium: 1168mg

Tabbouleh Salad

Prep Time: 20 minutes **Cooking time:** 15 minutes **Servings:** 4

If you want to lose weight, improve heart health or detox your system, this is the salad for you.

Ingredients:
2 C. water, filtered
1 C. millet, rinsed
⅓ C. extravirgin olive oil
Juice of 1 lemon
1 large garlic clove, crushed
1½ tsp. Himalayan pink salt, divided
2 large tomatoes, rinsed and finely diced
3 scallions, white parts only, rinsed and thinly sliced ½ English cucumber, rinsed and finely diced
¾ C. fresh mint, rinsed and finely chopped
1½ C. fresh parsley, rinsed and finely chopped

Directions:
Boil water over high heat. Add the millet and turn the heat to low.
Cover the pan and cook for 15 minutes.

Remove the pan from the heat and mash the millet with a fork. Let cool with the lid off for 15 minutes. It should be firm, but not crunchy or mushy.
Meanwhile, in a small bowl, whisk the olive oil, lemon juice, garlic, and ½ tsp. of salt. Let sit.
In a large bowl, combine the tomatoes, scallions, cucumber, mint, and parsley. Add the cooled millet. Pour the dressing over and mix well. Taste and season with the remaining 1 tsp. of salt, as needed.

NUTRITION: Calories: 3937 kcal Total Fat: 258 g Total Carbohydrates: 48 g Fiber: 88 g Sugar: 5 g Protein: 6 g

White Bean Chicken with Winter Green Vegetables

Servings: 8 **Cooking Time:** 45 Minutes

Ingredients:
4 Garlic cloves
1tablespoon Olive oil
3 medium parsnips
1kg Small cubes of chicken
1 Teaspoon cumin powder
2 Leaks & 1 Green part
2 Carrots (cut into cubes)
1 ¼ White kidney beans (overnight soaked)
½ Teaspoon dried oregano
2 Teaspoon Kosher salt Cilantro leaves
1 1/2tablespoon Ground ancho chilies

Directions:
Cook garlic, leeks, chicken, and olive oil in a large pot on a medium flame for 5 minutes.
Now add carrots and parsnips, and after stirring for 2 minutes, add all seasoning ingredients.
Stir until the fragrant starts coming from it.
Now add beans and 5 cups of water in the pot.
Bring it to a boil and reduce the flame.
Allow it to simmer almost for 30 minutes and garnish with parsley and cilantro leaves.

NUTRITION: Calories 263 Carbs: 24g Fat: 7g Protein: 26g

Rosemary and Garlic Sweet Potatoes

Prep Time: 10 Minutes **Cooking Time:** 15 Minutes **Servings:** 4

Ingredients:
2 tablespoons extravirgin olive oil
2 sweet potatoes (skin left on), cut into ½inch cubes 1 tablespoon chopped fresh rosemary leaves
½ teaspoon of sea salt
3 garlic cloves, minced
¼ teaspoon freshly ground black pepper

Directions:
In a big nonstick skillet over mediumhigh heat, heat the olive oil until it shimmers.

Supply the sweet potatoes, rosemary, and salt. Cook for 10 to a quarterhour, stirring occasionally until the sweet potatoes start to brown.

Put the garlic and pepper. Cook for 30 seconds, stirring constantly.

NUTRITION: Calories: 199Kcal Proteins: 2g Carbohydrates: 33g Fat: 7g

Breakfast Burgers with Avocado Buns

Prep Time: 10 minutes **Cooking time:** 5 minutes **Servings:** 1

Ingredients:
1 ripe avocado
1 egg, pastureraised
1 red onion slice
1 tomato slice
1 lettuce leaf
Sesame seed for garnish
salt to taste

Directions:
Peel the avocado and remove the seed. Slice the avocado into half. This will serve as the bun. Set aside.
Grease a skillet over medium flame and fry the egg sunny side up for 5 minutes or until set.
Assemble the breakfast burger by placing on top of one avocado half with the egg, red onion, tomato, and lettuce leaf. Top with the remaining avocado bun.
Garnish with sesame seeds on top and season with salt to taste.

NUTRITION: Calories 458, Total Fat 39g, Saturated Fat 4g, Total Carbs 20g, Net Carbs 6g, Protein 13g, Sugar: 8g, Fiber: 14g, Sodium: 118mg, Potassium 1184mg

Shrimp Pasta with Lemon and Garlic

Prep Time: 10 Minutes **Cooking Time:** 15 Minutes **Servings:** 3

Ingredients:
6 ounces (170 g) bean pasta
1 head broccoli, chopped into florets
3 tablespoons olive oil, divided
¾ pound (340 g) large shrimp, peeled and deveined 2 garlic cloves, minced
½ teaspoon salt
½ teaspoon freshly ground black pepper
Juice of 1 lemon
3 cups baby spinach

Directions:
Bring a large pot of water to a boil over high heat. Cook the pasta according to package instructions (usually 8 to 10 minutes). Add the broccoli for the final 2 minutes. Drain the pasta and broccoli and set them aside in the same pot they were cooked in.
Meanwhile, in a large skillet, heat 2 tablespoons of olive oil over medium heat. Add the shrimp and cook without turning for 5 minutes.
Add the garlic, then flip the shrimp to cook on the other side for 3 to 4

minutes, or until cooked through completely and pink in hue. Sprinkle the shrimp with the salt and pepper, add the lemon juice, and cook for 1 minute more.

Toss the pasta and broccoli with the remaining 1 tablespoon of olive oil.

Place 1 cup of baby spinach into each of 3 medium containers. Divide the broccoli and pasta into 3 large containers. Top each pasta container with a portion of shrimp.

NUTRITION: Calories: 436Kcal Proteins: 45g Carbohydrates: 32g Fat: 15g

Sweet Potato Chips

Prep Time: 20 minutes **Cooking Time:** 2 hours **Servings:** 6

Ingredients:
3 Tablespoons extravirgin olive oil
1 teaspoon of sea salt
2 larges thinly sliced sweet potatoes

Directions:
Power on the oven and heat it to 250°F. Place the rack in the center of the oven.

Take a large bowl and drop in the sweet potatoes' slices along with olive oil. Arrange the slices individually on 2 baking sheets—dust with the sea salt.

Lay the sheets inside the preheated oven and bake for about two hours; make sure to rotate the pans and flip the chips after 45 – 60 minutes.

As soon as the chips turn light brown and attain the crispiness, take them off the oven. Some may be a bit mushy, but they will again turn crisp as they begin to cool.

Let the chips cool for about ten minutes before serving. Serve straight away. The chips will again turn mushy after a few hours.

NUTRITION: Carbohydrate: 43g Protein: 7g Total Fat: 11g Calories: 268 Cholesterol: 0.0mg Fiber: 5g Sodium: 483mg

Strawberry Granita

Prep Time: 20 minutes **Cook time:** 0 minutes **Servings:** 8

Ingredients:
4 cups hot water
2 medium pitted dates
2 white tea bags (decaffeinated if children under twelve years old are served) 2 cups strawberries

Directions:
Place hot water in a suitable bowl or pitcher. Add dates and tea bags. Steep 20 minutes.
Remove tea bags. Cool.
Pour cooled tea and dates into blender. Add strawberries. Blend until smooth.
Pour blended mixture into a large glass casserole dish and place in freezer for almost 2 hours. (if frozen for much longer than that, it becomes harder to scrape.)
Remove from freezer and scrape thoroughly with a fork into small ice crystals. If bottom layers are not yet frozen enough to scrape, return to freezer for another hour and repeat scraping.
Serve in parfait cups.

NUTRITION: Calories 17; Fat 0.1g; Sodium 4mg; Carbs 3g; Fiber 0.9g; Sugars 1g; Protein 0.3g

Ruby Pears Delight

Prep Time: 10 minutes Cooking time: 10 minutes Servings: 4

Rich in antioxidants, dietary fiber and essential vitamins, pears are a good source of compounds to manage or curb inflammatory diseases.

Ingredients:
4 pears
26 oz. grape juice
11 oz. currant jelly
4 garlic cloves
Juice and zest of 1 lemon
4 peppercorns
2 rosemary springs
½ vanilla bean

Directions:
Pour the jelly and grape juice in your instant pot and mix with lemon zest and juice .
Dip each pear into the mix and wrap them in a clean piece of tinfoil, and place them orderly in the steamer basket of your instant pot.
Combine peppercorns, rosemary, garlic cloves, and vanilla bean to the juice mixture.
Seal the lid and cook at high for 10 minutes.
Release the pressure quickly, and carefully open the lid; bring out the pears, remove wrappers and arrange them on plates. Serve when cold with toppings of cooking juice.

NUTRITION: Calories: 4035 kcal Fat: 0.51 g Fiber: 98 g Carbs: 100.54 g Protein: 49 g

Pasta Primavera

Prep Time: 10 minutes Cooking Time: 20 minutes Servings: 4

Ingredients :
2 tablespoons unsalted butter
1 leek, white part only, thinly sliced
1 pound pencilthin asparagus, trimmed of woody ends and cut into ½
inch pieces
1 cup frozen green peas, thawed
1 teaspoon salt
¼ teaspoon freshly ground black pepper
½ cup white wine
2 cups vegetable broth or water
8 ounces glutenfree ziti
½ cup crumbled goat cheese cheese
2 tablespoons finely chopped fresh basil

Directions :
In a large pot, melt the butter over high heat.
Add the leek, asparagus, peas, salt, and pepper and sauté until softened, 1 to 2 minutes.
Add the wine and cook until it is reduced by half, 3 to 5 minutes.

Add the broth and ziti and bring to a boil. Cook, uncovered, until the ziti is tender, 10 to 12 minutes.
Add the cheese and stir until it melts into the ziti.
Sprinkle with the basil and serve.

NUTRITION: Calories: 409Total Fat: 11gTotal Carbohydrates: 55gSugar: 7gFiber: 10g Protein:17g Sodium: 1066mg

Tricky Cheesy Yellow Sauce
Servings: 2 **Cooking Time:** 0 Minutes

Ingredients:
1½ cups steamed, mashed cauliflower florets and hot ½ cup coconut milk, fullfat
½ cup nutritional yeast
1 tablespoon unsalted butter, ghee, or lard 1½ teaspoons coconut vinegar
1 teaspoon Himalayan salt, fine
1 teaspoon garlic powder

Directions:
Place all of the ingredients in a blender. Cover and blend on low, slowly bringing the speed up to high.
Continue to blend until the sauce is completely smooth. Taste for seasoning and add a little more salt and/or garlic powder if you like.
Store in an airtight container in the refrigerator for up to a week.
Warm in a saucepan on the stovetop over medium heat and stir occasionally.

NUTRITION: Calories: 185 ;Fat: 11g ;Protein: 11g;Carbs: 15g .

Fresh Tuna Steak and Fennel Salad
Prep Time: 15 minutes   **Cook time:** 25 minutes   **Serves** 4

Ingredients:
2 (1 inch) tuna steaks
2 tablespoons olive oil, 1 tablespoon olive oil for brushing 1 teaspoon crushed black peppercorns
1 teaspoon crushed fennel seeds
1 fennel bulb, trimmed and sliced
½ cup water
1 lemon, juiced
1 teaspoon fresh parsley, chopped

Directions:
Coat the fish with oil and then season with peppercorns and fennel seeds.
Heat the oil on a medium heat and sauté the fennel bulb slices for 5
minutes or until light brown. Add the water to the pan and cook for 10
minutes until fennel is tender. Stir in the lemon juice and lower heat to a simmer. Meanwhile, heat another skillet and sauté the tuna steaks for about 2 to 3 minutes each side for mediumrare. (Add 1 minute each side for medium and 2 minutes each side for medium well). Serve the fennel mix with the tuna steaks on top and garnish with the fresh parsley.

NUTRITION: Calories: 288   fat: 9g   protein: 44g   carbs: 6g   fiber: 2g   sugar: 3g   sodium: 105mg

Healthy Red Cabbage

Prep Time: 10 minutes **Cooking Time:** 20 minutes **Serve:** 4

Ingredients:
1 red cabbage head, sliced
3 tbsp canola oil
2 tbsp parsley, chopped
½ cup balsamic vinegar
Pepper
Salt

Directions:
Heat oil in a pan over mediumhigh heat
Add cabbage to the pan and sauté for 5 minutes.
Add vinegar, pepper, and salt and sauté for 15 minutes or until cabbage is cooked.
Garnish with parsley and serve.
4
NUTRITION: Calories 113 Fat 2 g Carbohydrates 7 g Sugar 9 g Protein 3 g Cholesterol 0 Mg

Easy Chicken and Broccoli

Prep Time: 10 minutes. **Cook time:** 7 minutes. **Serves:** 4

Ingredients:
3 tablespoons extravirgin olive oil
1½ pounds skinless chicken breasts, boneless, diced 1½ cups broccoli florets, or chopped broccoli stems ½ onion, chopped
½ teaspoon sea salt
⅛ teaspoon black pepper, freshly ground
3 garlic cloves, minced
2 cups cooked brown rice

Directions:
Cut the chicken breasts into bitesize pieces.
In a suitable skillet over mediumhigh heat, heat the olive oil until it shimmers.
Add the chicken, broccoli, onion, salt, and pepper. Cook for almost 7
minutes, while stirring occasionally, until the chicken is cooked.
Add the garlic. Cook for almost 30 seconds, while stirring constantly.
Toss with the brown rice to serve.

NUTRITION: Calories 389; Fat 19g; Sodium 198mg; Carbs 33g; Fiber 2g; Sugars 0.6g; Protein 28g

Sweet Potato and Butternut Squash Curry

Prep Time: 15 minutes **Cook time:** 15 minutes **Serves** 4 to 6

Ingredients:
1 tablespoon coconut oil
1 onion, chopped
1 large sweet potato, peeled and cut into ½inch cubes 2 cups (½inch) butternut squash cubes
2 garlic cloves, sliced

2 cups nosaltadded vegetable broth
1 (15ounce / 383g) can coconut milk
2 teaspoons curry powder
1 teaspoon sea salt
2 tablespoons chopped fresh cilantro

Directions:
Heat the coconut oil in a Dutch oven over high heat.
Add the onion and sauté for about 3 minutes until softened.
Stir in the sweet potato, butternut squash, and garlic and sauté for 3 minutes more.
Add the vegetable broth, coconut milk, curry powder, and salt to the vegetables, and bring to a boil.
Reduce the heat and bring to a simmer and continue cooking for about 5 minutes, or until the vegetables are forktender.
Sprinkle the cilantro on top for garnish and serve.

NUTRITION: calories: 122 fat: 5g protein: 2g carbs: 20g fiber: 3g sugar: 4g sodium: 671mg

Romesco Sauce with Vegetables and Sheet Pan Chicken

Prep Time: 26minutes **Total time:** 56minutes **Yield:** 4servings

Ingredients:
2 cubed Yukon gold potatoes
6 tbsps. olive oil
1 tsp. ground black pepper
½ tsp. salt
4 chicken thighs, bonein, and skinless
4 c. broccoli florets
1(7 oz.) jarred pepper, roasted ¼ c. slivered almonds
1 crushed garlic clove
1 tsp. paprika
½ tsp. ground cumin
¼ tsp. red pepper, crushed
2 tbsps. fresh cilantro, chopped

Directions:
Preheat your oven to attain 450°F. Add the 1/8 tbsp. salt, ¼ tbsp. black pepper, 1 tbsp. oil, and potatoes in a bowl and toss to combine. Transfer the potatoes to one side of a rimmed baking sheet. Add the ¼ tsp. pepper, chicken, 1 tbsp. oil, and 1/8 tbsp. salt into the same bowl and toss to coat.
Transfer the chicken to the other side of the baking sheet. Roast the chicken and potatoes for 10minutes. Meanwhile, add the broccoli, 2 tbsps. oil, ¼ tbsp. pepper, and 1/8 tbsp. salt inside a different bowl then tosses to mix. Add broccoli mixture to the potato side of your baking sheet and stir to mix.
Roast the broccoli for 15minutes. Meanwhile, add the roasted pepper, paprika, red pepper, cumin, almonds, ¼ tbsp. pepper, 2 tbsps. oil, 1/8 tbsp.

garlic and salt inside a food processor and process until a smooth consistency is achieved. Transfer the vegetables and chicken to a serving platter and sprinkle with the cilantro. Serve with roasted pepper sauce.

NUTRITION: Calories 499 Total fat 27g Carbs 30g Protein 33g

Zuppa Toscana

Prep Time: 15 minutes or fewer **Cooking Time**: 5 to 6 hours on low **Servings:** 46

Ingredients:
4 cups vegetable broth
2 cups chopped deribbed kale
2 small sweet potatoes, peeled and diced
1 medium zucchini, diced
1 (15ounce) can cannellini beans, rinsed and drained well 1 celery stalk, diced
1 carrot, diced
1 small onion, diced
½ teaspoon garlic powder
½ teaspoon sea salt
¼ teaspoon red pepper flakes
Freshly ground black pepper

Directions:
In your slow cooker, combine the broth, kale, sweet potatoes, zucchini, beans, celery, carrot, onion, garlic powder, salt, and red pepper flakes, and season with black pepper.
Cover the cooker and set to low. Cook for 5 to 6 hours and serve.

NUTRITION: Calories: 209Total Fat: 1gTotal Carbs: 43gSugar: 9gFiber: 10g Protein: 8g Sodium: 871mg

Healthy Broccoli Soup

Prep Time: 10 minutes **Cooking Time:** 3 hours **Serve:** 6

Ingredients:
8 cups broccoli florets
2 tbsp olive oil
6 cups vegetable stock
1 tbsp olive oil
2 tbsp ginger, chopped
4 cups leeks, chopped
1 tsp turmeric
1/8 tsp pepper
1 tsp salt

Directions:
Add broccoli and remaining ingredients into the pot and stir well.
Cover and cook on low for 3 hours.
Puree the soup using a blender until smooth. Season with pepper and salt.
Serve and enjoy.
NUTRITION: Calories 151 Fat 8 g Carbohydrates 19 g Sugar 1 g Protein 9 g cholesterol 0 mg

Shrimp and Mango Mix

Prep Time: 10 minutes **Cooking Time:** 0 minutes **Servings:** 5

Ingredients:
2 tablespoons Dijon mustard
3 tablespoons white wine vinegar
6 tablespoons avocado mayonnaise
4 cucumbers, peeled and cubed
1 mango, peeled and cubed
3 tablespoons chopped dill
1 pound shrimp, cooked, peeled and deveined
A pinch of salt and black pepper

Directions:
1. In a salad bowl, mix the cucumbers with the mango, shrimp, dill, salt and pepper and toss. Add the mustard, vinegar and mayonnaise and mix well then serve.

NUTRITION: Calories: 174Fat: 3Fiber: 2Carbs: 4

Lemon-Herb Tilapia

Prep Time: 15 minutes **Cooking Time:** 20 minutes **Servings:** 1

Ingredients:
2 6 oz. tilapia fillets
1 tsp dried tarragon
2 whole lemons
1 tbsp olive oil
1 tsp dried thyme
1 tsp kosher salt
1/2 tsp black pepper

Directions:
Preheat the oven to 350°F.
Combine the tarragon, thyme, kosher salt, and pepper in a small mixing bowl.
Set aside one of the lemons in thin slices (with skin on), carefully removing any seeds.
Cut the remaining lemon in halves and pour the juice over the tilapia filets, covering them evenly.
Season the tilapia on both sides with the dry herb seasoning combination.
In an ovensafe skillet over mediumhigh heat, heat the olive oil.
Cook the tilapia in the heated skillet for 35 minutes, or until golden brown. Flip the fish over and pour in more lemon juice from the half lemon. Place the lemon slices flat on the skillet and fish, then bake for 35 minutes, or until the fish is cooked through and flaky.
Garnish the fish with caramelized lemon slices.

Ginger-Broccoli Salad

Prep Time: 20 minutes **Cooking Time:** 0 minutes **Servings:** 3

Ingredients
¼ tsp sea salt
¼ tsp ground cinnamon

½ tsp ground turmeric
¾ tsp ground ginger
½ tbsp extra virgin olive oil
½ tbsp apple cider vinegar
2 tbsp chopped green onion
1/3 cup coconut cream
½ cup carrots, shredded
1 small head of broccoli, chopped

Directions
In a large salad bowl, mix well salt, cinnamon, turmeric, ginger, olive oil, and vinegar.
Add remaining Ingredients, tossing well to coat.
Pop in the ref for at least 30 to 60 minutes before serving.

NUTRITION: Calories: 113Total Fat: 10gSaturated Fat: 2gTotal Carbs: 5gNet Carbs: 3g Protein: 2gSugar: 1gFiber: 2g Sodium: 233mgPotassium: 198mg

Oregano Dressing on Salad Greens

Prep Time: 15 minutes **Cooking Time:** 0 minutes **Servings:** 4

Ingredients
1/3 cup chopped red onion
¾ cup crumbled soft fresh goat cheese
1 ½ cups diced celery
1 ½ large red bell peppers, diced
4 cups baby spinach leaves, coarsely chopped
1 tbsp chopped fresh oregano
2 tbsp fresh lemon juice
2 tbsp extra virgin olive oil

Directions:
In a large salad bowl, mix oregano, lemon juice and oil.
Add pepper and salt to taste.
Mix in red onion, goat cheese, celery, bell peppers and spinach.
Toss to coat well, serve and enjoy.

NUTRITION: Calories: 91Total Fat: 4gSaturated Fat: 0gTotal Carbs: 11gNet Carbs: 5g Protein: 6gSugar: 3gFiber: 6g Sodium: 207mgPotassium: 720mg

Chocolate-Coated Banana

Time: 20 minutes **Serving Size:** 12   **Prep Time:** 20 minutes **Cook Time:** 0 minutes
This one is easy and treats you to your favorite popsicle dip even on this diet, because all the ingredients used possess curative powers that help control chronic inflammation.

Ingredients:
1 cup almonds rubbed in chili powder, coarsely chopped
1 cup pistachios, coarsely chopped
1 cup hazelnuts, coarsely chopped
3 cups dark chocolate chips
1 tbsp white coconut oil

6 large bananas
Dried and chopped berries of your choice

Directions:
Peel, cut bananas in half and insert a popsicle stick to the end that is cut. Place the fruits on a lined tray and freeze for 20 minutes.
Next, melt the chocolate with the oil over a low flame, and stir until it becomes smooth. Then pour it into a bowl large enough to dip the bananas.
Take out the bananas and line up your chocolate and chopped nuts, as well as the fruit.
Take a large piece of parchment paper on which you will arrange the bowls with the berries, nuts and chocolate.
Now, dip a banana in the chocolate mix and sprinkle it with the nuts, and if you like, the berries too. Alternate between types of nuts and berries until you have coated all 12 halves.
Place each coated banana back on the tray, and freeze for about 10-20 minutes before enjoying your treat.

NUTRITION: Calories 210 Carbs 25 g Fat 14 g Protein 14 g Fiber 14 g

Refreshing Apple Smoothie

Prep Time: 5 minutes **Cooking Time:** 5 minutes **Serve:** 1

Ingredients:
1 medium apple, chopped
¼ tsp ground ginger
¼ tsp cinnamon
1 scoop vanilla protein powder
¾ cup spinach
1 ½ cups unsweetened almond milk

Directions:
Add chopped apple and remaining ingredients into the blender and blend until smooth and creamy. Serve immediately and enjoy.

NUTRITION: Calories 184 Fat 5 g Carbohydrates 35 g Sugar 23 g Protein 2 g Cholesterol 0 mg

Delicious Mango Smoothie

Prep Time: 5 minutes **Cooking Time:** 5 minutes **Serve:** 1

Ingredients:
1 cup mango chunks
¼ tsp turmeric
1 tsp vanilla
1 banana
½ cup orange juice
1 scoop vanilla protein powder
1 cup unsweetened almond milk

Directions:
Add mango chunks and remaining ingredients into the blender and blend until smooth and creamy.

Serve immediately and enjoy.
NUTRITION: Calories 314 Fat 4 g Carbohydrates 67 g Sugar 47 g Protein 4 g Cholesterol 0 mg

Healthy Spinach Smoothie

Prep Time: 5 minutes **Cooking Time:** 5 minutes **Serve:** 2

Ingredients:
1 1/2 cups fresh spinach
½ cup ice
1 ½ cups cashew milk
1 pear, cored & diced
1/4 banana
½ cup water

Directions:
Add pear and remaining ingredients into the blender and blend until smooth and creamy.
Serve immediately and enjoy.

NUTRITION: Calories 77 Fat 7 g Carbohydrates 15 g Sugar 8 g Protein 1 g Cholesterol 0 mg

Full Coconut Cake

Prep Time: 5minutes   **Total time:** 50minutes   **Yield:** 4servings

Ingredients:
3 eggs, yolks, and whites
¾ c. Coconut Flour
separated
½ tsp. Coconut Extract
1 ½ c. warm Coconut Milk
½ c. Coconut Sugar
2 tbsp. melted Coconut Oil
1 c. Water

Directions:
Beat the whites until soft form peaks. Beat in the eggyolks along with the coconut sugar. Whisk in coconut extract and coconut oil. Gently fold in the coconut flour.
Line a baking dish and pour the batter inside. Cover with aluminum foil.
Pour the water inside your Instant Pot. Put the container in the pressure cooker. Close the lid and cook for 45minutes in MANUAL mode. Do a quick pressure release. Serve and enjoy.

NUTRITION: Calories 350, Carbohydrates 47 g, Fiber 5 g, Fat 11 g, Protein 5 g

Blueberry Crisp

Prep Time: 15 minutes   **Cook time:** 20 minutes   **Serves** 4

Ingredients:
½ cup coconut oil, melted, plus additional for brushing 1 quart fresh blueberries
¼ cup maple syrup
Juice of ½ lemon

2 teaspoons lemon zest
1 cup glutenfree rolled oats
½ teaspoon ground cinnamon
½ cup chopped pecans
Pinch salt

Directions:
Preheat the oven to 350ºF (180ºC). Brush a shallow baking dish with melted coconut oil. Stir together the blueberries, maple syrup, lemon juice, and lemon zest in the dish. In a small bowl, combine the oats, ½ cup of melted coconut oil, cinnamon, pecans, and salt. Mix the ingredients well to evenly distribute the coconut oil. Sprinkle the oat mixture over the berries.
Place the dish in the preheated oven and bake for 20 minutes, or until the oats are lightly browned.

NUTRITION: Calories: 497 fat: 33g protein: 5g carbs: 51g fiber: 7g sugar: 26g sodium: 42mg

Vanilla Coconut Cake

Prep Time: 15 minutes   **Cook time:** 45 minutes   **Serves** 8

Ingredients:
½ cup coconut oil, melted, plus more for greasing the baking dish 2 cups egg whites (about 12), at room temperature Pinch sea salt
1 cup unsweetened almond milk
6 tablespoons raw honey
2 teaspoons pure vanilla extract
1 cup coconut flour
½ cup shredded unsweetened coconut
2 teaspoons baking powder

Directions:
Preheat the oven to 350ºF (180ºC).
Lightly grease a baking dish with coconut oil and set it aside.
In a large bowl, beat the egg whites and sea salt with an electric mixer until soft peaks form. Set them aside.
In another large bowl, whisk the almond milk, honey, remaining ½ cup of coconut oil, and the vanilla. Whisk in the coconut flour, coconut, and baking powder until well combined.
Fold the beaten egg whites into the batter, keeping as much volume as possible, until just blended.
Spoon the batter into the prepared dish and smooth the top.
Bake the cake for about 45 minutes, or until cooked through and lightly browned.
Cool the cake completely on a wire rack.
Serve with fresh fruit, if desired.

NUTRITION: Calories: 237 fat: 17g protein: 7g carbs: 16g fiber: 1g sugar: 15g sodium: 136mg

Chocolate Bananas

Prep Time: 5 Minutes **Cooking Time:** 15 Minutes **Servings:** 4

Ingredients:
3 Bananas, large & cut into thirds
12 oz. Dark Chocolate

1 tbsp. Coconut Oil

Directions:
To begin with, melt the chocolate and coconut oil in a double boiler for 3 to 4 minutes or until you get a smooth and glossy mixture.
Next, keep the popsicles into the end of each of the banana by inserting it.
After that, immerse the chocolate into the warm chocolate mixture.
Shake off the excess chocolate and place them on parchment paper.
Sprinkle with the topping of your choice.
Finally, place them in the freezer for a few hours or until set.

NUTRITION: Calories: 427Kcal Protein:9g Carbohydrates: 80g Fat: 16g

Sweet Porridge Dessert

Prep Time: 10 minutes **Cooking Time:** 30 minutes **Servings:** 4

Ingredients
For the porridge:
1 ½ cups coconut milk
½ cup steel cut oats
½ cup water
2 black tea bags
1 teaspoon vanilla extract
2 tablespoons raw honey
For the acai berry ripple:
2 tablespoons acai powder
1 cup berries
1 tablespoon maple syrup
For the pistachio cream:
¼ cup pistachios, roasted
½ cup coconut milk

Directions
Put ½ cup water in a pot and heat up over medium heat. Add oats, vanilla extract, tea bags and 1 and ½ cups coconut milk. Stir well, bring to a simmer, cover and cook for 30 minutes. Discard tea bags then add honey, stir well and take off heat. In a blender, puree 1 cup berries with acai powder and maple syrup then transfer to a bowl. In the same blender, add ½ cup coconut milk and pistachios and puree. Divide oats into bowls, add acai ripple and top with pistachios cream then serve.
Enjoy!

NUTRITION: Calories: 140Fat: 4Fiber: 2Carbs: 6Protein: 5

Mini Spinach Muffins

Servings: 12 Muffins **Cooking Time:** 15 Minutes

Ingredients:
2 cups packed spinach
¼ cup raw honey
1 teaspoon vanilla extract

3 tablespoons extravirgin olive oil
2 eggs
1 cup almond flour
1 cup oat flour
1 teaspoon baking soda
2 teaspoons baking powder
½ teaspoon salt
Pinch freshly ground black pepper

Directions:
Preheat the oven to 350ºF (180ºC). Line a 12cup muffin pan with paper muffin cups.
Put the spinach, honey, vanilla, and olive oil in a food processor, then break the eggs into it. Pulse to mix well until creamy and smooth.
Combine the flours, baking soda, baking powder, salt, and black pepper in a large bowl. Stir to mix well.
Make a well in the center of the flour mixture, then pour the spinach mixture into the well. Stir to mix well.
Divide the batter into muffin cups, then arrange the muffin pan in the preheated oven and bake for 15 minutes or until a toothpick inserted in the center comes out clean.
Remove the pan from the oven. Allow to cool for 10 minutes, then serve immediately.

NUTRITION: calories: 107; fat: 8g ; protein: 2g ; carbs: 19g ; fiber: 0g ; sugar: 5g ; sodium: 216mg

Lemon Ginger Broccoli and Carrots

Servings: 6 **Cooking Time**: 5 Minutes

Ingredients:
1 tablespoon avocado oil
1" fresh ginger, peeled and thinly sliced
1 clove garlic, minced
2 broccoli crowns, florets
2 large carrots, sliced
½ teaspoon kosher salt Juice from
½ large lemon
¼ cup of water

Directions:
Put the oil to the inner pot. Heatup within 2 minutes.
Add the ginger and garlic and sauté 1 minute. Add the broccoli, carrots, and salt and stir to combine. Turn off.
Add the lemon juice and water and use a wooden spoon to scrape up any brown bits—Cook within 2 minutes.
Serve immediately.

NUTRITION: Calories 67 Fat: 2g Protein: 3g Sodium: 245mg Fiber: 3g Carbohydrates: 10g Sugar: 3g

A simple pudding sweetened with peanut butter

Prep Time: 10 minutes **Cooking time:** 0 minutes **Servings:** 4

Ingredients
⅛ tsp. nutmeg, ground
½ C. peanuts, raw and unsalted
⅛ tsp. salt, iodized
⅓ C. pumpkin puree
¼ tsp. cinnamon, ground
⅛ C. pure maple syrup
¼ C. almond milk, unsweetened
½ tbsp. coconut oil, melted
⅛ cloves, ground

Directions:
Pulse nutmeg, peanuts, salt, pumpkin puree, cinnamon, maple syrup, almond milk, coconut oil, and cloves for approximately 3
minutes.
Make sure all ingredients are incorporated. Divide equally into individual glasses or a dish.
Serve immediately and enjoy!

NUTRITION: Calories: 1518 kcal Fat: 89 g Fiber: 36 g Carbs: 153 g Protein: 99 g 29

Rice Pudding

Prep Time: 5 minutes **Cooking time:** 20 minutes **Servings:** 4

Rice is fiber packed with macronutrients good for the body.

Ingredients
4 ⅓ C. almond milk, unsweetened
3½ oz. brown rice
2 tbsp. pure maple syrup, separated

Directions:
Empty milk in a saucepan on the highest heat setting. As it starts to bubble, turn heat to medium/low, then transfer the rice into the pot.
Toss to cover the rice completely. Toss frequently for 20 minutes or until it reaches the desired thickness.
Transfer to serving dishes and drizzle each with ½ tbsp. maple syrup.

NUTRITION: per serving Calories: 1514 kcal Fat: 92 g Fiber: 0.89 g Carbs: 216 g Protein: 55 g

Quick Fish Bowl

Prep Time: 11minutes **Total time:** 26minutes **Yield:** 2servings

Ingredients:
2 tilapia fillets
1 tbsp. olive oil
1 avocado
1 tbsp. ghee butter

1 tbsp. cumin powder
1 tbsp. paprika
2 c. coleslaw cabbage, chopped
1 tbsp. salsa sauce
Himalayan rock salt, to taste
Black pepper to taste

Directions:
Heat the oven to 424F. Using a foil, line a baking sheet. Puree the avocado.
Using olive oil, brush the tilapia fillets and season with spices and salt.
Grease with the ghee butter and put the fish onto the baking sheet.
Let it bake for 15minutes, then remove it from the heat. Allow it to cool for 5minutes. Mix and gently toss the salsa sauce and the coleslaw cabbage in a bowl. Add the mashed avocado, season with pepper and salt Cut the fish and add to the bowl. Bake for 1415minutes. Serve hot.

NUTRITION: Carbs: 5,2 g Fat: 24,5 g Protein: 16,1 g

Quinoa Salmon Bowl

Prep Time: 15 minutes **Cook time:** 0 minutes **Serves** 4

Ingredients:
4 cups cooked quinoa
1 pound (454 g) cooked salmon, flaked
3 cups arugula
6 radishes, thinly sliced
1 zucchini, sliced into half moons
3 scallions, minced
½ cup almond oil
1 tablespoon apple cider vinegar
1 teaspoon Sriracha or other hot sauce (or more if you like it spicy) 1 teaspoon salt
½ cup toasted slivered almonds (optional)

Directions:
Combine the quinoa, salmon, arugula, radishes, zucchini, and scallions in a large bowl. Add the almond oil, vinegar, Sriracha, and salt and mix well.
Divide the mixture among four serving bowls, garnish with the toasted almonds (if using), and serve.

NUTRITION: Calories: 790 fat: 52g protein: 37g carbs: 45g fiber: 8g sugar: 4g sodium: 680mg

Manhattan-Style Salmon Chowder

Prep Time: 10 minutes **Cook time:** 15 minutes **Serves** 4

Ingredients:
¼ cup extravirgin olive oil
1 red bell pepper, chopped
1 pound (454 g) skinless salmon, pin bones removed, and chopped into ½ inch pieces
2 (28 ounces / 794 g) cans crushed tomatoes, 1 drained and 1 undrained 6 cups nosaltadded chicken broth

2 cups diced sweet potatoes
1 teaspoon onion powder
½ teaspoon sea salt
¼ teaspoon freshly ground black pepper

Directions:
In a large pot over mediumhigh heat, heat the olive oil until it shimmers.
Add the red bell pepper and salmon. Cook for about 5 minutes, stirring occasionally, until the fish is opaque and the bell pepper is soft. Stir in the tomatoes, chicken broth, sweet potatoes, onion powder, salt, and pepper.
Bring to a simmer and reduce the heat to medium. Cook for about 10
minutes, stirring occasionally, until the sweet potatoes are soft.

NUTRITION: Calories: 570 fat: 39g protein: 41g carbs: 55g fiber: 16g sugar: 24g sodium: 600mg

Almond & Chia Bites with Cherries
Servings: 2 **Cooking Time**: 20 Minutes

Ingredients:
1 cup cherries, pitted
1 cup shredded coconut
¼ cup chia seeds
¾ cup ground almonds
¼ cup cocoa nibs

Directions:
1. Blend cherries, coconut, chia seeds, almonds, and cocoa nibs in a food processor until crumbly. Shape the mixture into 24 balls and arrange on a lined baking sheet. Let sit in the fridge for 15 minutes. Serve and enjoy!

NUTRITION:
Per Serving: Calories: 95;Fat: 2g;Protein: 4g;Carbs: 22g.

Impressive Parfait with Yogurt, Berry, And Walnut
Servings: 2 **Cooking Time:** 0 Minutes

Ingredients:
2 cups plain unsweetened yogurt, or plain unsweetened coconut yogurt or almond yogurt
2 tablespoons honey
1 cup blueberries, fresh
1 cup raspberries, fresh
½ cup walnut pieces

Directions:
1. Whisk the yogurt and honey in a medium bowl. Spoon into 2 serving bowls.
2. Top each with ½ cup blueberries, ½ cup raspberries, and ¼ cup walnut pieces.

NUTRITION: Per Serving: Calories: 505 ;Fat: 22g ;Protein: 23g ;Carbs: 56g .

Quinoa & Spinach Salad

Prep time: 10 minutes. **Cooking time:** 0 minutes. **Servings:** 2

Ingredients:
16 ounces quinoa, cooked
1 handful raisins
1 handful baby spinach leaves
1 tablespoon maple syrup
½ tablespoon lemon juice
½ Tablespoon olive oil
1 teaspoon ground cumin
Sea salt and black pepper, a pinch
½ teaspoon chili flakes

Directions:
1. Toss the quinoa with spinach, raisins, cumin, salt, and pepper in a mixing bowl. Toss in the maple syrup, lemon juice, oil, and chili flakes, then serve as a breakfast side dish.
2. Enjoy!
NUTRITION: Calories: 170 Fat: 3 g Fiber: 6 g Carbs: 8 g Protein: 5 g

Winter Style Fruit Salad

Servings: 6 Cooking Time: 0 Minutes

Ingredients:
- 4 cooked sweet potatoes, cubed (1-inch cubes) 3 pears, cubed (1-inch cubes)
- 1 cup of grapes, halved
- 1 apple, cubed
- ½ cup of pecan halves
- 2 tablespoons of olive oil
- 1 tablespoon of red wine vinegar
- 2 tablespoons of raw honey

Directions:
1. Mix the olive oil, red wine vinegar, then the raw honey to make the dressing, and set aside.
2. Combine the chopped fruit, sweet potato, and pecan halves, and divide this between six serving bowls. Drizzle each bowl with the dressing.
NUTRITION: Total Carbohydrates 40g Dietary Fiber: 6g Protein: 3g Total Fat: 11g Calories: 251

Limey Cilantro with Shrimp Salad

Prep time: 10 minutes **Cook time:** 5 minutes **Serves** 1

Ingredients:
6 ounces shrimp, peeled and deveined
2 cups mixed greens
1 avocado, pitted, peeled, and diced
1 scallion, finely sliced
¼ cup Cilantro Lime Vinaigrette

Directions:

Fill a small pot with filtered water and bring to a boil. Add the shrimp and cook for 2 or 3 minutes, until they turn pink and become opaque. Using a strainer, drain the shrimp and immediately rinse under cold running water until they're cool to touch.

Put the mixed greens in a salad bowl. Top with the avocado, scallions, and cooked shrimp.

Drizzle the dressing onto the salad and toss to combine. Enjoy right away.

NUTRITION: Calories: 629   Fat: 47g   Protein: 32g   Total Carbs: 31g   Fiber: 19g   Net Carbs: 12g

Snow Pea and Watermelon Salad

Prep time: 25 minutes   **Cook time:** 0 minutes   **Serves** 4

Dressing:
½ cup olive oil
¼ cup apple cider vinegar
2 tablespoons raw honey
1 teaspoon freshly grated lemon zest (optional) Pinch sea salt

Salad:
4 cups (½-inch) watermelon cubes
1 English cucumber, cut into ½-inch cubes
1 cup halved snow peas
1 scallion, white and green parts, chopped
2 cups shredded kale
1 tablespoon chopped fresh cilantro

Make the Dressing

In a small bowl, whisk the olive oil, cider vinegar, honey, and lemon zest (if using). Season with sea salt and set it aside.

Make the Salad

In a large bowl, toss together the watermelon, cucumber, snow peas, scallion, and dressing.

Divide the kale among four plates and top with the watermelon mixture.

Serve garnished with the cilantro.

NUTRITION: calories: 353   fat: 26g   protein: 4g   carbs: 30g   fiber: 3g   sugar: 20g sodium: 8mg

40 Day Meal Plan

B. Breakfast **L.** Lunch **D.** Dinner

Day 1
B. Walnut and Banana Bowl
L. Lemongrass and Ginger Mackerel
D. Sweet Potato Chips

Day 2
B. Sweet Potato Oat Bars
L. Capellini Soup with Tofu And Shrimp
D. Ruby Pears Delight

Day 3
B. Eggs With Cheese
L. Bean Shawarma Salad
D. Tricky Cheesy Yellow Sauce

Day 4
B. Milk and Creamy Yogurt Bowl
L. Jicama Black Bean Salad
D. Healthy Red Cabbage

Day 5
B. A Quick antipasto pasta
L. Creamy Turkey with Mushrooms
D. Sweet Potato and Butternut Squash Curry

Day 6
B. Orange Oatmeal Muffins
L. Energy Bites
D. Zuppa Toscana

Day 7
B. Coconut Rice with Berries
L. Almond-Orange Torte
D. Shrimp and Mango Mix

Day 8
B. Snow Pea and Watermelon Salad
L. Apple, Berries, and Kale Smoothie
D. Ginger-Broccoli Salad

Day 9
B. Breakfast Porridge
L. Brown Rice and Shitake Miso Soup with Scallions
D. Strawberry Granita

Day 10
B. Healthy Chia Pudding
L. Chicken and Brussels sprouts
D. Pasta Primavera

Day 11
B. Fruit and Millet Breakfast
L. Cod and Quinoa Mix
D. Fresh Tuna Steak and Fennel Salad

Day 12
B. Breakfast and Brunch Mushroom Crepes
L. Cherry-balsamic Chicken Breasts
D. Easy Chicken and Broccoli

Day 13
B. Spiced Morning Chia Pudding
L. Shirataki Pasta with Avocado and Cream
D. Romesco Sauce with Vegetables and Sheet Pan Chicken

Day 14
B. Golden Milk
L. Banana Pops
D. Healthy Broccoli Soup

Day 15
B. Blueberry Breakfast Blend
L. Raspberry and Chard Smoothie
D. Lemon-Herb Tilapia

Day 16
B. Breakfast Porridge

L. Orange Banana Alkaline Smoothie
D. Oregano Dressing on Salad Greens

Day 17
B. Healthy Chia Pudding
L. Easy Pork Chops
D. Beef, Pork, and Lamb Thai Beef with Coconut Milk

Day 18
B. Breakfast and Brunch Mushroom Crepe
L. Beets Gazpacho
D. Fake Mushroom Risotto

Day 19
B. Golden Milk
L. Chicken Lettuce Wraps
D. Rosemary Pork Chops

Day 20
B. Coconut Rice with Berries
L. Shrimp Pasta with Lemon and Garlic
D. Slow Cooker Shawarma

Day 21
B. A Quick antipasto pasta
L. White Bean Chicken with Winter Green Vegetables
D. Pork Sausage

Day 22
B. Coconut Rice with Berries
L. Beef and Mushroom Pasta
D. Chai Pudding

Day 23
B. Orange Oatmeal Muffins
L. Cabbage Soup
D. Spinach Soup with Gnocchi

Day 24
B. Breakfast Porridge
L. Honey Mustard Chicken
D. Ginger Honey Pork Chops

Day 25
B. Fruit and Millet Breakfast
L. Mushroom Squash with Vegetable Soup
D. Mini Spinach Muffins

Day 26
B. Fruit and Millet Breakfast
L. Vegan "Frittata"
D. Berry Bliss Slow Cooker Pork

Day 27
B. Spiced Morning Chia Pudding
L. Baked Butternut Squash Rigatoni
D. Chicken with Fennel and Zucchini

Day 28
B. Blueberry Breakfast Blend
L. Lemongrass and Ginger Mackerel
D. Mushroom Risotto

Day 29
B. Orange Oatmeal Muffins
L. Rosemary and Garlic Sweet Potatoes
D. Garlicky Lamb Stew

Day 30
B. Milk and Creamy Yogurt Bowl
L. Tabbouleh Salad
D.

Day 31
B. Blueberry Breakfast Blend
L. Chicken with Snow Peas and Brown Rice
D. Lemon and Mint Breezy Blueberry

Day 32
B. Golden Milk
L. Cheddar & Kale Frittata
D. Meatballs

Day 33
B. Spiced Morning Chia Pudding
L. Baked Navy Beans
D. Quick & Juicy Lamb Chops

Day 34
B. Sweet Potato Oat Bars
L. Jicama Black Bean Salad
D. Salmon and Feta Cheese and Papillote

Day 35
B. Eggs With Cheese
L. Massaged Swiss Chard Salad with Chopped Egg
D. Healthy Tuna Salad

Day 36
B. Milk and Creamy Yogurt Bowl
L. Bean Shawarma Salad
D. Grilled Eggplant Salad

Day 37
B. Orange Oatmeal Muffins
L. Chicken and Brussels sprouts
D. Nutritious Salad with Lentil And Beets

Day 38
B. Blueberry Breakfast Blend
L. Cod and Quinoa Mix
D. Veggie Salad

Day 39
B. A Quick antipasto pasta
L. Capellini Soup with Tofu And Shrimp
D. Blackberry Salad

Day 40
B. Coconut Rice with Berries
L. Brown Rice and Shitake Miso Soup with Scallions
D. Carrot and Raisin Salad

Manufactured by Amazon.ca
Bolton, ON